High Praise for *Trans*

"What a great gift this book will be i
Memories is like a comforting walk
friend—three friends in fact. The three authors are so brave, so
candid, so experienced, and so encouraging in how they work
through issues from their own pasts. Their example is a beacon
of encouragement for anyone who has experienced challenge or
trauma and wants to hunker down to work through their own
memories."

—Gillian Deacon, author of *Naked Imperfection* and
There's Lead in Your Lipstick

"We each have moments from our past that jolted us from the
innocence of childhood into a sometimes unforgiving reality.
This is a book of such moments. Through guided writing exercises, the authors do an exceptional job of aiding their readers
to write about their moments and, through such writing, find
meaning and bring healing to old wounds."

—Donna Morrissey, award-winning author of five
adult novels, including her recent bestseller,
The Fortunate Brother

"It's miraculous that deep in the human psyche and spirit is a
force of healing–waiting, ready to push us towards surprising
insights and transformation. With guidance, with intention, we
can release this amazing potential. These three wise women–
through their honesty, open hearts and wisdom–can be your
guides. Let the alchemy begin when the first words appear at
the tip of your pen."

—Rob Rutledge, MD, author of *The Healing Circle*,
Chair, and CEO of HealingandCancer.org

"What is exciting about this book is that it doesn't just tell us what to do; it shows us with examples coupled with suggestions and prompts. This is memoir in action where the reader will experience intimate stories from the authors' lives as they make their own discoveries. Perhaps because so much has been shared by the writers, it feels as if a safe space has been created and anyone attempting a similar journey into their past will be held and supported within the suggested structure."

—Paul Dodgson, UK playwright, musician,
and creative writing tutor

"*Transforming Memories* is a powerful testimony to the personal transformation that can begin when one finds the courage to take a flying leap across the chasm of isolation and silent self-judgment to a place where curiosity about the self one might become has a chance to flourish. Compassion, for ourselves and for and from others, helps us find that courage. Some embark on this journey of self-realization alone, others, like the authors, find strength in a trusted community. There is no map for this uniquely personal journey, but the authors offer some tools and resources one can use along the way. These are tools that just might enable one, in the words of the poet John O'Donohue, 'To live the life that I would love.'"

—Beth A Lown, MD, Associate Professor of Medicine,
Harvard Medical School and Mount Auburn
Hospital; and Medical Director, The Schwartz Center
for Compassionate Healthcare

Transforming Memories

Sharing Spontaneous Writing
Using Loaded Words

Liz Crocker
with
Polly Bennell & Holly Book

Bull Publishing Company
Boulder, Colorado

Bull Publishing Company
P.O. Box 1377
Boulder, CO 80306
Phone (800) 676-2855 / Fax (303) 545-6354
www.bullpub.com

Distributed in the United States by Independent Publishers Group, 814 N. Franklin Street, Chicago, IL 60610

Library of Congress Cataloging-in-Publication Data

Names: Crocker, Liz, author. | Bennell, Polly, author. | Book, Holly, author.

Title: Transforming memories : sharing spontaneous writing using loaded words / Liz Crocker with Polly Bennell & Holly Book.

Description: Boulder, Colorado : Bull Publishing Company, [2016] | Includes bibliographical references and index.

Identifiers: LCCN 2016034288 (print) | LCCN 2016042117 (ebook) | ISBN 9781936693924 (softbound : alk. paper) | ISBN 9781945188053 (ePub) | ISBN 9781945188060 (mobi)

Subjects: LCSH: Graphotherapy. | Creative writing--Therapeutic use.

Classification: LCC RC489.W75 C76 2016 (print) | LCC RC489.W75 (ebook) | DDC 616.89/1663--dc23

LC record available at https://lccn.loc.gov/2016034288

Manufactured in the United States of America

22 21 20 19 18 17   10 9 8 7 6 5 4 3 2 1

Interior design and production by Dovetail Publishing Services
Cover design and production by Shannon Bodie, Lightbourne, Inc.

We dedicate this book to our parents, who gave us gifts even through their pain, and to all those who are suffering in silence.

Contents

We explain the choice of the title and subtitle, highlight discoveries we made as we wrote and shared memories of our alcoholic parents and childhoods, reflect on who this book is for, and offer thoughts about how to approach both the examples of writing and the prompts for readers to try spontaneous writing and sharing themselves.

We describe the nature and benefits of spontaneous/expressive writing along with some of the research that supports the value of writing about traumatic experiences and painful memories. In addition to the power of writing, we underscore the importance of sharing and listening along with thoughts about how to begin such a journey.

The three of us, with our common bond of having grown up with an alcoholic parent, explain how we found ourselves engaged in a process of spontaneous writing, then gathering to share our memories and experiences.

We reflect on the significance of childhood years affected by having an alcoholic parent and then present our three original pieces of writing, which showcase significant images from our childhood memories.

Chapter 4   The List—Our Loaded Words 53

We originally generated a long list of sixty-eight "loaded words" to serve as prompts for spontaneous/expressive writing and ultimately chose fourteen of them. The ensuing writings are presented along with relevant dictionary definitions and short commentaries about each word.

Chapter 5   Your Turn 131

We invite readers to consider writing themselves and provide suggestions and prompts for writing exercises to act as catalysts for self-discovery.

Contents

Introduction

You have to be brave with your life so
that others can be brave with theirs.

—Brené Brown

What's In a Title?

The three of us—Liz, Polly, and Holly—were all daughters of alcoholics. We met together and wrote and shared our memories, first with each other and now with you, in hopes of better understanding and healing our own pasts and also in hopes of helping others who have suffered from similar experiences.

We thought we were simply writing to create a book that might be helpful to other children of alcoholics, but, ultimately, we found ourselves in a larger process of deep reflection that was profound, healing, and transforming.

Prompted in part by words that held loaded meaning for us, we spontaneously wrote. *Transforming Memories* is a collection—part memoir, part how-to—of our writings, along with an invitation to others, whatever their past burdens, to use the technique of spontaneous writing to address painful memories.

Choosing a title for this book was a challenging process. We kept asking ourselves, "Should our title be short and mysterious, or should it be detailed and specific?" We wanted a title that would be catchy, that would give some indication about the key elements of the contents, and that would have both general appeal to anyone who has experienced challenges in their childhoods as

1

well as specific relevance for children of alcoholics. Because the various words of our title and subtitle were chosen with great thought, we want to deconstruct them so you can understand and appreciate our choices.

"Transforming Memories"

The word "transforming," in grammatical terms, can be both an active verb and a descriptive adjective. The term is active if used in a sentence such as, "As we wrote and shared, we were actually *transforming our memories*, often difficult ones, from our past." "Transforming" can also be descriptive, as in this sentence: "The act of reflecting on and writing about what we remembered from our childhoods changed painful memories into *transforming memories, memories* that were shape-shifting."

And what are "memories"? They are snapshots or internal movies from times past and, if joyful, are to be savored and shared with others. However, if memories are painful or trigger feelings of confusion or shame or emptiness, they are typically not shared, but held in place, burrowed uncomfortably in our hearts and minds.

The beauty of the term "transforming memories," being both an adjective and a verb, is that it captures both what we did and what effect our process had. Our childhood memories had been transforming for us as children; they shaped our view of ourselves and how we understood the world at the time. Through writing and sharing, we were able to transform these secretive and painful images and interpretations to ones that are now open to the light, accepted and less painful.

"Sharing"

We wrote and then shared our writing with each other. Both the writing and the sharing helped us learn more about each other and also about ourselves. And now we have chosen to share what we wrote with you, hoping you will be inspired to try your own writing.

"Spontaneous Writing"

"Spontaneous writing" is a term used to describe a discipline of writing about traumatic events that is done quickly, without forethought. The technique is also referred to as "expressive writing" or "therapeutic writing."

We learned that the healing effects of spontaneous writing are not trivial—in fact, there is growing evidence that translating stressful events into written language can improve both brain and immune functions. Someone put it best when they said, "If you write it down, the weight of it is on paper, not on your heart."

"Loaded Words"

The word "loaded" has three common meanings:

1. slang for "drunk," "intoxicated," or "under the influence of alcohol";

2. charged with emotional or associative significance; and

3. bearing or having a full load.

We created a list of "loaded words," words we felt to be powerful in evoking memories of living with an alcoholic parent, and used them as prompts for our spontaneous writing. These words were "loaded" for us—loaded in that they emerged from our memories of growing up in households "under the influence" of alcohol; loaded in terms of the strong emotional overtones and connotations they triggered in us beyond their literal meanings; and loaded in terms of representing both the memory burdens we carried from our childhoods with an alcoholic parent and the extra responsibilities and secrets we shouldered.

We learned how the power of language can impact our lives to harm or to heal. Every day, our lives are filled with words that may seem harmless on the surface but can trigger deep reactions, causing us to cry, to lash out in anger, to withdraw into sadness or judgment, or to feel afraid or unseen. Writing is a powerful tool to appreciate the poignancy of simple words and to communicate, first with oneself and then with others.

Discoveries

After doing our various spontaneous writing exercises and then sharing them, we identified some key aspects of our process, including the following:

- ❖ Using our single loaded words as spontaneous writing prompts, we were able to remember things more specifically than we thought we could.

- ❖ Writing turned out to be a "way in" to the deeper places in ourselves.

- ❖ The act of reading what we'd written out loud to each other turned out to be powerful in its own right, helping us reach beyond the facts of our experiences to touch in to our emotions of the moments.

❖ Even though we had been good friends before we started this journey together, we learned so much more about each other as we shared memories and listened to each other's stories.

❖ We chose to break the silence and secrecy of our childhoods—the alcoholic parent we couldn't talk about—and honestly explore feelings we might have had but had buried. It felt comfortable and safe to explore our pasts with others who had, in their own ways, "been there."

❖ We realized we were not crazy to feel the way we did or to have some of the personality quirks we had developed in childhood and carried with us as adults—such as a need to control, a fear of being abandoned, and a gnawing doubt about our worthiness.

❖ Being engaged in a creative process such as spontaneous writing enabled us to "lose our minds and come to our senses"—quite a feat for those of us who habitually try to control things, tend to live in our heads a lot, and spend time trying to figure out everything for everyone else.

Our purpose, in all the writing we did, was to discover/ uncover ourselves in order that we might increase our appreciation of what happened to us (or didn't) and enhance our perceptions of what occurred. Even though we may have written some critical-sounding comments, our purpose was never to blame, only to describe and understand.

Who Is This Book For?

Although our process of writing and sharing was centered on our common bond of having an alcoholic parent, we know that alcohol abuse in a family is not the only experience that sets up feelings of abandonment or fear or a sense of emptiness or constant guardedness. We believe this book is relevant not just for those with an alcoholic parent but for anyone who has experienced challenges or trauma in childhood.

In *Adult Children of Alcoholics*, one of the earliest books on this subject written in 1983, Janet Woititz explains that her book was written only with children of alcoholics in mind but that the characteristics common to children of alcoholics can also be found among those who grew up with such circumstances as compulsive behaviors (such as gambling, drug abuse, or eating extremes, which can also be referred to as food addictions), chronic illness, profound religious attitudes, or foster care. She says, "It appears that much of what is true for the children of alcoholics is also true for others, and this understanding can help reduce the isolation of countless persons who also thought they were 'different' because of their life experience."

Similarly, Herbert L. Gravitz and Julie D. Bowden, in their book *Recovery: A Guide for Adult Children of Alcoholics*, published in 1985, observed that "children of alcoholics are but the visible tip of the iceberg." The authors refer to other "children of trauma," adding to Woititz's list with categories such as survivors of war and genocide, chronic mental illness, physical and sexual abuse, or extremely judgmental/perfectionist/critical environments.

Irrespective of the unique details of your early years, we hope our writings will help you feel you are not alone. *Transforming Memories* is first an opportunity to journey with us. Second, it is an invitation to consider some of the strong memories from your own past, using the power of spontaneous writing to help you unpack those memories and reveal them more explicitly to yourself so that sharing and healing can take place.

How to Approach *Transforming Memories*

Transforming Memories is not a typical self-help book—providing a simple recipe for what to do to heal. It is also not meant, in any way, to be a group pity party. We had no interest in blaming others or looking for sympathy, only in describing memories and deepening our understanding of the legacies of our pasts. This book is simply an unfiltered sharing of writing and process, how we scratched the surface of the pain in our hearts and souls and how we explored some of the darker shadows.

While this book is not a group memoir per se, it does contain some of our individual memories. And while the examples of writing come from us, the book is not intended to be about us as much as it aspires to be about what you might be moved to try for yourself.

We invite you to learn about both our process and our discoveries: see how we generated spontaneous writing exercises; appreciate that a single word can trigger very different perspectives from different people; wonder what *you* might write if you picked one of our loaded words and just put your pen to paper or fingers to the keyboard for ten minutes; contemplate what words would spark memories for you; imagine the possibility of gathering with just one trusted friend or even a small group of others who share your background and with whom you feel comfortable and safe enough to write and share.

Transforming Memories seeks to be different in its simplicity. You can simply read what's here, or you can explore the possibilities of using words to spark your own memories, or you can go talk to a friend and tell him or her something you've not shared before. No rules! All you need is curiosity about potential discoveries.

Do you have to have experienced trauma, illness, disability, or dysfunctional relationships to appreciate this book? Will these stories make you feel sad? Will the reflections make you fearful of trying to explore your own subconscious? Can there be benefit from experimenting with the power of language even from happy memories? Of course, we can't know the answers to these questions, because they are questions for you.

What we can say is that we are grateful for the journey we took together, and that the journey has transformed us and helped us be grateful for our lives, both then and now. We understand that our journey is not over as we continue to discover the significance of our pasts, try to practice loving kindness to ourselves and others, and surrender to and accept what comes our way.

We heartily affirm the spirit with which Socrates made the bold statement that "the unexamined life is not worth living." We looked back; we turned memories over to see their undersides; we examined the habits and patterns in our lives to understand where they came from and to appreciate we could change them; we questioned our assumptions; and we embraced reasons to appreciate our own worthiness.

We no longer want to hide from our pasts or pretend we are not who we are. We agree with the lines from Tennyson's poem "Ulysses" in which he said, "I am a part of all that I have met . . .

and yet experience is an arch wherethrough gleams the untravelled world whose margin fades for ever and for ever when I move . . ."
Who would we be now if we had not been who we were?

We have to face the pain we have been running from. In fact, we need to learn to rest in it and let its searing power transform us.
—Charlotte Joko Beck

1

Good for Your Health: Writing, Gathering, and Sharing

*Write it down, girl. Tell everyone how much
it hurts. Sharing will make it easier to bear.*
—Terri Jewell

A Healthy Journey

When we decided to get together and give ourselves spontaneous writing exercises to access our memories and our emotions about our alcoholic parents and childhoods, we had no idea how profound and useful this process would be for us. We certainly had no idea that research would lend credence to and understanding about how writing and sharing are good for one's health.

Storytelling was the first significant human technology—fire came later! From the oldest practices of recording thoughts and events in songs and spoken stories to later practices such as diaries, journals, ballads, and letters, and even newer examples of memoirs, blogs, chat rooms, and Facebook postings, personal storytelling is the central way we relate to each other. As humans, we are designed for connecting with one another. We have used stories as the most common vehicle to communicate who we are and to find out who you are. For years, people have used writing, therapeutically, to make sense of their stories of illness, of grief, of abuse and oppression.

In our case, we *wrote* because we wanted to create a book and writing was something we knew how to do. We *got together* because we had wanted to generate a collaborative project. We wrote about the scenes and legacies caused by alcoholism in our families because we were willing to break the secrecy and silence of our pasts to try to make sense of our experiences in the safety of our group. And so, we also *wanted to share*, first with each other and now with you, because we could still feel the powerful hold on us created by alcoholism and we wanted to lighten our burdens.

Writing and sharing can be "course corrections" if one is troubled by the way things are unfolding in one's life. Maya Angelou said, "I write in order to discover myself." We believe the act of sharing our past experiences, first in writing and then with others, helped us discover hidden truths about ourselves, to appreciate and honor our pasts, to recognize our basic goodness, and to begin to let go of the painful memories and self-deprecating assumptions of our long-held stories.

What Is Spontaneous/Expressive Writing?

We referred to our writing exercises with our loaded words as "spontaneous writing"—identifying a word, setting the clock for ten or twenty minutes, and then saying "Go!"

We particularly liked the word "spontaneous" because it reminded us we were to just write and not stress about it. At the time, we didn't know that "expressive writing" and "therapeutic writing" were also accepted terms for essentially the same process. In the research literature, the term "expressive writing" is most commonly used, but the spontaneous part of the practice is very important.

Whatever term is being used, though, the intentions and guidelines are generally the same and very simple:

❖ Just write . . . without pre-thought or judgment or concern about spelling, punctuation, or grammar.

❖ Write about an event or events you associate with stress or trauma (past or present) or something that troubles you in some way.

❖ Write continuously for a short period of time, ten to twenty minutes.

❖ Write frequently, ideally every day for several days.

There is something quite liberating in writing quickly, without a predetermined plan or an internal (and often critical) editor. Many of us typically find it hard to live in the moment, but spontaneous writing, with a clock ticking for ten to twenty minutes, brings us to "right now."

We hope that you will be inspired to try such spontaneous/expressive writing yourself. At any point in reading this book, feel free to put it down and take ten minutes to capture something that comes into your head or heart. Start by just writing or at least making some notes to remind you of your spontaneous thoughts or feelings or memories to return to at a later time. We've provided a number of writing prompts later, in chapter 5—titled "Your Turn"—but you don't have to wait . . . you can start now.

For us, our loaded words were like lightning rods, attracting energy that cracked us open, taking us to deeper places in ourselves. We may have thought we didn't remember much from our childhoods, but writing had a way of unlocking our souls' storage units, full of memories, images, and feelings that we had tended to lock away.

What we didn't know during the various times we got together, writing and sharing, is that there is a growing body of evidence that supports the healing power of spontaneous/expressive writing and group process. It has been gratifying to learn that others recommend writing and sharing as a process to enhance one's health; it was what we simply chose to do.

The Benefits of Spontaneous/Expressive Writing

Writing enables people to create order out of the chaos of memories, to lighten the load of situations that cause stress, and to apply a healing balm to emotional pain. The products of writing are valuable, not just for the writer but also for those who love the writer. Through the writer's words, loved ones can often learn and understand more about their friend/family member and become better able to offer empathy and compassion.

Writing is used as a therapeutic approach in mental health programs and in hospitals with patients dealing with physical and/or mental illnesses. In university departments, writing programs enhance students' self-awareness and self-development. People who have experienced any form of trauma often create narratives of their stories to help them see their experiences more clearly.

A 2005 article in *Advances in Psychiatric Treatment* by Karen Baikie and Kay Wilhelm, titled "Emotional and Physical Health Benefits of Expressive Writing," summarized the benefits, which include the following:

❖ Fewer stress-related visits to the doctor and fewer days in the hospital

❖ Improved immune system functioning

❖ Reduced blood pressure

❖ Improved lung and liver function

❖ Improved mood, reduced symptoms, and decreased worries in depressed individuals

❖ Reduced absenteeism from work and quicker reemployment after job loss

❖ Improved memory

More recent studies have identified additional benefits of expressive writing, including the following:

❖ Wounds heal faster

❖ Reduced viral load and increased level of virus-fighting immune cells in HIV-positive patients

❖ Reduced levels of stress hormones

❖ Improved satisfaction among soldiers returning home from war zones

An article in the *New York Times* on January, 19, 2015, titled "Writing Your Way to Happiness," talked about the vast array of scientific research studies on the benefits of expressive writing. The article specifically talks about the positive effects of writing to improve mood disorders, reduce symptoms in cancer patients, improve health after a heart attack, and boost memory.

Details of these and other selected studies about the benefits of writing are included in appendix A.

How or Why Does Spontaneous/Expressive Writing Work?

Why is spontaneous/expressive writing potentially so beneficial? One theory, first voiced by Dr. James Pennebaker from the University of Texas, is that actively *inhibiting* thoughts and feelings about trauma requires significant effort and leads to cumulative stress. The effort of not dealing with traumatic events can stress the body and lower defenses, thereby leading to physical symptoms of illness or intrusive and worrisome thoughts.

Writing about trauma can relieve emotional pressure and, therefore, reduce overall stress on the body. One particular by-product of reducing stress is that one's ability to sleep is improved, and it has been shown that people who sleep at least seven hours a night heal faster than those who get less sleep.

Writing can help us make sense of past experiences and confused or painful emotions. As we write, we often remember missing details of clouded events and begin to integrate these new details into old memories, helping us make sense of what happened in the past and providing revised understanding of old wounds.

Traumatic memories are often jumbled and incoherent and just sit inside of us, trembling with confusion and circular repetition. Putting words on paper is like putting a brake on a series of endlessly repeating storylines, troubled thoughts, or near-obsessive ruminations—which frequently happen in the wee hours of the night.

Henriette Anne Klauser, author of *With Pen in Hand: The Healing Power of Writing*, says, "The act of consigning the hurricane inside your head to paper quiets the agitated spirit, shifts the brain waves, brings peace. It takes what can be toxic and decontaminates it. It makes it safe. Writing makes sense of confusion and gives voice to the wisdom within."

Spontaneous/expressive writing can get us out of our heads and into our hearts and help us visit our "emotional habit cage" with a fresh perspective. This can lead to a revised, integrated, and coherent story about previously experienced events. It is not so much that this kind of writing is cathartic as it is likely to be integrative, to bring order and increased perspective to memories.

Louise DeSalvo, in her book *Writing as a Way of Healing*, says:

> We receive a shock or a blow or experience a trauma in our lives. In exploring it, examining it, and putting it into words, we stop seeing it as a random, unexplained event. We begin to see the order behind appearances.
>
> Expressing it in language robs the event of its power to hurt us; it also assuages our pain. And by expressing ourselves in language, by examining these shocks, we paradoxically experience delight—pleasure even—which comes from the discoveries we make as we write, from the order we create from seeming randomness or chaos.
>
> Ultimately then, writing about difficulties enables us to discover the wholeness of things, the connectedness of human experience. We understand that our greatest shocks do not separate us from humankind. Instead, through expressing ourselves, we establish our connection with others and with the world.

Writing may not solve every problem one has, but writing has the potential to lead the writer to different perspectives. Putting your words on paper doesn't mean you will forget what happened or how you felt—but new views of long-held interpretations may make more sense and may feel less heavy. Writing helped us understand many experiences anew. We hope you will take up our invitation to try similar writing and sharing and will experience the same benefits.

Beyond Writing—Sharing and Listening

Many of the studies about the benefits of spontaneous/expressive writing are specific about *writing*, as opposed to just *talking*. This does not mean that telling our stories to others does not have value—in fact, telling stories to each other creates a sense of community and helps us transcend isolation that separates us from each other, often leaving us feeling less lonely and alienated. Research shows that people who feel lonely or isolated have three to five times the risk of premature death from all causes when compared to those who have a sense of connection and community.

Through our original writings and our loaded words, we *wrote* about our memories before we *spoke* them. The act of writing was personal and private, touching places in our brains and heart, without judgment. It is possible that we were able to reveal and contemplate deeper truths by first writing.

But we were also a group, and we met together and shared our writing, often reading aloud. This act of speaking and giving literal voice to experiences and feelings that had been largely unexpressed was often emotional in and of itself. But we had created a safe container for ourselves. We trusted that each of us would listen openly and with compassion and that we would be fully heard.

Sometimes, as we read something we'd written or shared reactions to people or events, we didn't necessarily see how we were repeating old patterns, but the others did. Through simple comments and questions such as "What you've said feels so familiar—you've mentioned this before," "Can you tell me more about . . . ?", or "Does this remind you of anything?" we were further revealed to ourselves. And every time we listened to each other, we listened somewhat into ourselves. What a gift!

Henry David Thoreau said, "It takes two to speak the truth—one to speak and one to hear." However, not everyone is a good listener. Some people appear to be listening but are really in their heads, not listening but getting ready to make their own point. Being a good listener takes curiosity and discipline—to not interrupt and to be fully present, listening not only with both ears, but also with your eyes to observe the speaker's body language, facial expressions, breathing patterns. Listening takes us beyond spoken words, listening for what is not said. For us, listening *deeply* was a sign of unconditional respect and was an important and key ingredient of our creating a context of safety.

We learned that we needed not only to listen to each other, but also to ourselves. Through our writing, through using the gift of words, we were doing important work of accessing memories and feelings. It was important to learn to quiet the voices in our own heads and listen to our physical and emotional responses. This is what one person meant when she said, "I've learned the difference between the questions 'Can you talk about it?' and 'Can you feel about it?'"

How to Begin?

Perhaps for you, such sharing may feel scary, like walking on emotional quicksand. Our recommendation is to start as we did—by just telling your own story to yourself through your own writing. See what happens when you decant significant memories. The simple act of writing may be enough, as a start, and the research would tell you that the act of writing is good for your health.

As a next step, if you feel ready, identify someone with whom you are comfortable—a dear friend, a wise colleague, someone from a group you belong to that is based on shared experiences or values—and ask if she or he would be willing to read what you've written, to be a witness to something about you that is important. While you might feel nervous, the person you reach out to will likely feel honored. Your request may well be perceived as a gift.

Our experience of sharing with others was positive, right from the very beginning. We felt less alone, and that was comforting. Consider this reflection from our very first gathering: "We instinctively understood one another—our stories were different, but the impacts tended towards being universal. We saw and heard ourselves in the lives of others. We may have come from different places, but we all knew about bumpy rides, uncertain destinations, and what it feels like to be left on the side of the road. But it was about more than just recognizing the similarity of our scars; it was the acknowledgement of our goodness, our triumph over adversity. And we've done more than just survive—we have emerged as good people, caring professionals and parents, and contributing community members."

The three of us shared a common bond of mutuality, of both sympathy and empathy, based on our knowledge that each of us had had an alcoholic parent. This initial foundation of common experience created enough trust for us to write and then share our original stories. Over many months, as we continued to write, gather together, and share, we were able to get the best of all possible worlds. Our process, described in the next chapter, was as rich and profound as it was because we wrote *and* we talked *and* we listened.

To write about what is painful is
to begin the work of healing.
—Pat Schneider

Chapter 2

Our Process
Sparks from a Common Bond

*And the day came when the risk to remain tight in a
bud was more painful than the risk to bloom.*

—Anaïs Nin

How does a book like this come together? How can we capture
the players, the substance, the process? How can we distill such a
profound, shared journey into a few pages?

A journalistic tool, in conveying elements of a story, is to
examine the who, what, when, where, and why. So here's what we
would say if this were a news story.

Who? . . . Three Women with a Common Bond

The three of us—Liz and Polly and Holly—met some time ago,
when we all had young children. As we got to know each other,
we learned we had something in common: that each of us had
grown up with an alcoholic parent. We met others with alcoholic
parents and a group of seven of us went away for a weekend
retreat to talk about our memories as children of alcoholics and to
consider writing a book together of shared experiences.

Over time, four people from this group dropped out for different reasons, including time, the difficulty of examining one's
own pain, not wanting to invade family privacy, and not wanting

to risk criticizing or hurting parents who were still alive. Although we missed their involvement, if we had learned anything as children of alcoholics, we knew we had to honor and respect their choices.

The three of us have gently held those four, as well as so many other people, in our hearts as we journeyed together—parents (alcoholic and otherwise), siblings, friends, people we've met along the way with similar childhood experiences, and people who've had different childhoods but who have also struggled with issues of abandonment or emotional or physical neglect.

What? . . . We Thought We Were Writing a Book, but It Was Much More

At the very beginning, before the three of us ever met as a group, we simply wrote, independently, on our own, unfettered, about some key memories and/or strong images from our childhoods. There were no rules or expectations.

When we reviewed what each of us had written, we were struck with the details and the emotions that each of us had revealed. We became more committed to the belief that a book of such reflections could be helpful to others, especially given that, at the time, there were very few books about or for children of alcoholics.

As a group, we generated a list of loaded words that sparked memories and emotions, deciding to use the technique of spontaneous writing, writing for ten to twenty minutes, to explore how these words touched us. We experimented with the word "hope" and were impressed with what we were able to create from nothing in such a short space of time.

And so, we chose more words from our list; we went away and wrote; then we got together again to share our writings and talk about what was happening in our lives in terms of events and emotional discoveries. Then we chose more words and wrote some more; we got together again and shared more about ourselves . . . and then we let years go by and let our project stall.

Years later, when we reconvened, as we looked back on our loaded words and our gatherings, we were reconvinced that the work we'd done might be useful to others. We understood that our *process* of unpacking our once-painful memories through writing and sharing was every bit as important as the writings that had been our focus years before. We acknowledged that our childhoods still influence our views of the world and some of our habitual responses but that our journey of writing and sharing had led to helpful insights, new perspectives, and a lightening of our feelings of shame and confusion.

When? . . . Then and Now and All the Years In Between

The first spark of conversation about the legacies of living with an alcoholic parent occurred many years ago as we were first getting to know each other. Our active period of writing and gathering together and sharing took place over a couple of years as we worked in different ways, at different times—alone and together.

Between then and now, we can see that we continued to benefit from that active period, fueled by what we learned about our pasts and how we carried certain habitual responses into adulthood, by how safe and understood we felt, by knowing we were not alone.

We firmly believe that things happen in the fullness of time, but, that being said, we are surprised that our journey from then to now has encompassed so many years. Nonetheless, we believe that this project unfolded when it did, at specific and different times over the decades, when we were somehow "ready"—ready to write, ready to reveal and share with each other, ready to learn and grow and surrender, and ready to invite you to journey with us and then try your own hand at writing.

Where? . . . Here and There and Everywhere

Most of us wrote while we were at home, but coffee shops also saw some pens flying across pages or keyboards clicking away. Our group gatherings always took place "away," meaning in no one person's home but rather at inns or B&Bs.

Being away from our normal day-to-day lives removed distractions and allowed space for full emotional expression. Being away helped us focus, be truly present with each other, to speak from our hearts and listen deeply to each other with compassion. Being away also provided some anonymity in the places we stayed—we were simply guests. Little did the various innkeepers know we were igniting sparks to light our way on our healing pathways.

Why? . . . Because Everyone Has a Right to Heal but May Not Know How

We thought it would be useful to others to write a book about the reflections of children of alcoholics. Alcoholism is so very prevalent—it is an equal-opportunity destroyer in all demographics, and it affects the entire family. As such, being a child of an alcoholic creates an array of significant legacies. Growing up in an alcoholic or other manifestation of a dysfunctional family can be traumatic and is typically not talked about, even among family members.

Even outside of one's family, when one person reveals to another that they are the child of an alcoholic, a common response is, "I thought it was just me; now I can see I am not alone." Through writing assignments and sharing our lives and our emotions with each other, we found we were engaged in a deep and healing process. We wanted to offer this to others.

Someone who read an early version of our work encouraged us to continue, to create a book. She told us:

> As an adult child of an alcoholic who's never read a book on the topic, it was an enthralling and reassuring read . . . reassuring because I'm just beginning to understand how my own dysfunctional behaviors are common among ACOAs?* and not simply "my fault." I felt I was being welcomed into a conversation, that I belonged, that judgment was left outside the room.

From our perspectives, we know that being silent about the difficult experiences of being a child of an alcoholic can feed a sense of shame, a continuing need to try to control one's universe, and a persistent fear of abandonment along with basic doubts about feeling safe or loved. We have chosen to break the silence, to write and speak to each other and now to you.

---

* Adult Children of Alcoholics. ACA is a more recent evolution of the term ACOA and also refers to 'adult children of alcoholics.'

When we started our journey, we had no idea that research would prove the significant value of writing to heal past traumas. At the time, these studies were just beginning to emerge but now, increasingly, there are numerous articles and books that document and illustrate how creating written narratives can help you make sense of your life. It is clear that writing, along with sharing and listening, is good for your health.

We can transform our memories. Healing can start with a simple conversation, especially if that conversation touches and uncovers a common bond of childhood secrets and pain. It only takes a spark to start a fire. Hopefully, the reflections of our childhoods, through our original writings in the next chapter, will inspire you to reach for your own match.

Be patient toward all that is unsolved in your life. And try to love the questions themselves. Do not seek the answers that cannot be given to you, because you would not be able to live with them. This journey we call life is not always clear. And the point is to live everything. Live the questions now. Perhaps you will gradually, without noticing it, live along some distant day into the answer.

—Rainer Maria Rilke

Chapter 3

Childhood Snapshots— Original Writings

When we share our writing, someone else knows what we've been through. Someone else cares. Someone else has heard our voice. Someone else understands. We learn that we are no longer alone and that we no longer need be alone.

—Louise DeSalvo

Childhood

Childhood represents a time when the world is new and exciting, full of things and people and adventures to experience and enjoy. Just think of the delight a young child has when he or she learns to walk for the first time or discovers that covering one's eyes and saying "peek-a-boo" reveals someone still there or that ducks will come to you on a lake if you have cracked corn.

Children are typically nurtured through food and shelter, love and physical comfort, a sense of safety, and continual messages that "you are special." As a result, children tend to be optimists, tend to deny or avoid unpleasant realities, and have a cheerful outlook on life. They enjoy acquiring increasing knowledge, competence, and, in later years, the recognition and acceptance of peers.

However, when a child grows up in a family with alcoholism or other form of addiction or abuse, the natural positive outlook

29

of childhood can be smothered or stamped out. Sometimes circumstances require a child to take on adult-like responsibilities rather than freely play; to struggle to make sense of situations that are confusing or frightening or unpredictable; to question whether he or she is the cause of the family dysfunction; to wonder if he or she is worthy of love or can ever be "good enough."

If a child is ashamed of his or her family, approaching adolescence and the desire to be accepted by peers creates new pressures of needing to keep the "family reality" a secret and to pretend that everything is "normal" at home. In the words of Janet Woititz, author of *Adult Children of Alcoholics*, "When is a child not a child? When the child lives with alcoholism."

Our Childhoods

Before we originally gathered as a group, we each wrote about a memory or memories from our childhoods. There were no rules, and the three "original writings" ended up being very different in length, style, and content. Of course, this was no surprise given that the three of us are unique adults, with our own writing voices and styles of expression. However, while our original writings were dissimilar in style, in many ways there were more similarities than differences in our childhoods.

We all had siblings (but each of us were in different places in birth order—an oldest, a youngest, and a second of four); we all grew up in houses and in cities (Montreal, Quebec, and Canton and Cleveland, Ohio); we all experienced the death of a parent when we were young (ages eight, fifteen, and twenty-eight); we all acquired at least one stepparent; none of us ever talked about the big things that were happening in our lives, such as alcoholism, accidents, and death; and we all could cite the age at which we felt our childhoods ended—one at eight, one at eleven, and one at twelve!

The material comforts of our childhood years did not translate into the far more fundamental, important, and emotional comfort of feeling loved or, in some cases, feeling safe. None of us were aware of any reasons to worry about money during our childhoods, but we still felt huge emotional holes as a result of our childhood experiences. In the midst of having food and shelter, we still experienced a deep sense of neglect. None of us can imagine how much more difficult and complicated—materially and emotionally—things would have been with known financial stresses added to the equation.

These original writings present poignant snapshots into three childhoods—those of Liz Crocker, Polly Bennell, and Holly Book. The writings of each author are marked in the text as **L**, **P**, and **H**. They stand on their own as glimpses into three different lives that had the common bond of having an alcoholic parent. Even though the three styles of writing and ways of conveying significant aspects of our childhoods are very different, they helped us know ourselves and each other more deeply.

We invite you into our worlds as children.

—\\\\\\—

L It was winter, I was in grade six, and it was the night of the school carnival when the announcement would be made as to which group had won the ice sculpture contest. I was very excited because three of us had worked hard creating a snow and ice rendition of "Gus-Gus," the cute little mouse from Walt Disney's *Cinderella*.

I remember feeling so happy and proud when we heard we had won first prize. When my father came to pick me up, I was still beaming. He came to see Gus-Gus and seemed pleased for us. When we got home, I went running into the house and upstairs to tell my mother. She was drunk. I know it wasn't the first time, but it was the first time I realized she was "a drunk." Too, because I'd been so excited about wanting to share something with her that I had accomplished, the reality of her staggering and slurring state was devastating. I felt the bright colors of my world become grey.

This night marks, for me, the beginning of a period of time in my life that was characterized by phenomenal unpredictability and a roller coaster of emotions. Strangely enough, I arrived at school the next day to discover that my favorite striped scarf, which had been wound around Gus-Gus' neck, had been stolen. Life seemed pretty unfair.

Looking back, I feel my childhood ended at twelve. The years from twelve to fifteen were rough. At some level, I knew my mother loved me but I was confused—how could someone so lovely and loving also be so drunk and unable to speak clearly and fall down and yell and scream and hit my father? And while I'm sure my father loved me too, I don't remember him telling me so and we never talked about what was going on, day by day, week by week, year by year.

A Pool of Blood

I remember waking up in the middle of the night and hearing a low moan coming from my mother's room. Somewhat frightened, I went down the hall and found my mother lying on the floor in a pool of blood. I got a face cloth, helped her up, and gently wiped the blood off her face. It looked like she had broken her nose because it was twisted on her face. My father, a busy and successful lawyer, was out of town on a business trip and my sister was at boarding school. I didn't really know what to do and then remembered Elsie, our live-in maid. Even though it was 1:30 a.m., I woke her up and between us we called the doctor and sat with my mother.

Apparently my mother had combined alcohol with some pain medication she had for some dental surgery and had fallen trying to get to the bathroom. I silently hoped that every time she looked at the cast on her nose and her black eyes, she would somehow know how awful that night was for me and make sure it never happened again.

In fact, over the next couple of years, my mother broke her nose again, but at least it wasn't at night and there was no low moan or pool of blood. She also broke her back and her shoulder and her foot in various other falls. Somehow I became numbed to these experiences.

Dinner

There was a sense of normalcy every night at the dinner table but it was a thin veneer. The table was always beautifully set with place mats and silver and a good meal prepared (likely by Elsie). A fly on the wall would have seen two adults and one child sitting at the table eating. But if the fly really looked carefully, it would have seen that the child spent her first few minutes cutting up the food on her mother's plate to accommodate the mother's difficulty moving a knife and fork in a coordinated way. The fly would have also noted that the mother didn't eat much and that conversation seemed stilted and awkward. Invariably the mother and father would start to argue and the child would eat in silence.

No Clothes

For some reason, my mother would spend a lot of time before actually going to bed wandering around upstairs with no clothes on. I remember one night in particular, when she sat on the floor beside my bed, naked, with the lights on, long after I was supposed to go to sleep. I don't think I really paid attention to what she was saying because I kept wishing she would go to bed. I was a teenager then and it just seemed she should at least have some clothes on. On that night, and others like it, when she would finally leave my room, I would hear her screaming accusations at my father about affairs with other women. I have no idea whether her accusations were true, but I couldn't help but think that if they were, I wouldn't blame him. I can't imagine she was a very romantic sight. She had been such a beautiful and vibrant woman in her younger years and now she was naked and drunk.

The Glow of a Cigarette in the Dark

Our garage was attached to our basement and sometimes we stored things in the garage. I can't even remember what I was going to get, but I remember being in the garage late one night and not bothering to turn on the light because I could see well enough with the bit of light coming through the door from the basement. I went around the front of the car to the other side of the garage. As I turned to come back into the house, I saw the glow of a lit cigarette inside the car. My immediate reaction was one of absolute terror, thinking there was robber, or worse still, a rapist, lying in wait for me. In an instant (that seemed like forever), I realized that it was my mother, slumped in the seat behind the wheel, drinking from a bottle and smoking. I think I must have screamed at her, because I'd been so afraid and now was so mad. She screamed back to leave her alone. I did.

A Family Picnic

My parents and I went to visit my sister at boarding school on a fall Sunday and we all went into the countryside somewhere for a picnic. I recall having a pleasant time even though a picture taken that day haunts me even now. It is of my sister, in her boarding school uniform; with one hand, she is twirling a plastic glass on the end of a stick and with the other, she is holding up a bottle of Gordon's gin. A cigarette dangles from the corner of her mouth. I know she was just goofing around but her playful scene was what I saw daily, for real. I still have the photograph even though I hate it.

A Glimmer of Hope

It was a weeknight and my mother and I were home alone. She was reasonably sober and we were talking in the kitchen. Somehow the subject of Alcoholics Anonymous came up. I remember becoming alert in every pore of my body and thinking this conversation must proceed carefully. Finally, she said, "I know that's what I should do. Will you please call them for me?" Somehow, I knew I shouldn't and said, "I wish I could but you have to be the one to call. I'll look up the number for you though." I went into the hallway to get the phone book, praying with all my might that she wouldn't change her mind. She didn't. She called. I was so proud of her in that moment.

"He Didn't Come"

Coming home from school one afternoon, I found my mother in her bedroom, standing by her bureau, dressed in a beautiful, tailored, red suit, looking out the window. Hearing me come into the room, she said, "He didn't come." I asked, "Who didn't come?" and she just repeated, "He didn't come." It was as though she was in a trance and all she could do was repeat that phrase. To this day, I don't know who "he" was but only know that I detected a huge sense of sadness and disappointment in my mother's voice that afternoon. She'd been sober for a while and I felt so terrible for her, when she was trying so hard, that something had happened to make her unhappy. I was scared, too, that whatever and whoever it was might drive her back to drinking again.

Peter Piper Picked a Peck of Pickled Peppers

Peter Piper was my first boyfriend. There's no question that anyone named Peter Piper is going to be teased about his name a lot, and one has to wonder what his parents were thinking of when they picked the name Peter instead of any other name. As a general rule, I was somewhat reluctant to bring friends home, never knowing what the situation would be, but usually I warned people. Bringing home a boyfriend was a much bigger deal. The first time Peter came home with me, I just hoped for the best. Luck was not with me. My mother greeted us at the door. She was drunk and began to recite a slurred version of "Peter Piper picked a peck of pickled peppers," which is difficult to say even if you're sober. Peter laughed. I was mortified.

"Where Does Mohair Come From?"

I can't recall whether I'd stayed home from school or whether my mother had been taking an afternoon nap, but I have a strong image of cuddling in bed with her under a mohair blanket. It was a special time, cozy and warm, not necessarily talking about anything of consequence. I used to wish these moments could be frozen in time and that she'd never drink again. Fingering the blanket, I asked her, "Where does mohair come from?" With a twinkle in her eye, she replied, "From baby 'moes,' I guess." The image of what a baby mo might look like sent both of us into hysterics and we laughed until tears ran down our faces.

I Should Have Been There

One year, after Christmas, I visited a friend in Buffalo and had a marvelous time skating, seeing sights, dating boys, and living in a functional family for a few days. When I got home, I discovered that my mother had fallen and broken her foot. Somehow, I felt I should have been home for that—I certainly shouldn't have been away somewhere having a good time. I'm not sure why I felt so responsible, but I did and no one told me otherwise. I never took another trip away from my family until after my mother's death.

Valentine's Day

I never figured out how she did it because she'd been drunk for days on end, but I remember this Valentine's Day that my mother gave everyone in the family the cutest cards. The fact that this woman whose life was such a wreck was also a woman who was extremely thoughtful touched a resonating chord in my being. I remember feeling warm all over that day and loving her so much for caring. The next day, it occurred to me that she might well have been driving drunk to get the cards, and the warm feeling turned cold.

My Favorite Meal

When I was twelve, I had a hip operation and was in the hospital for three weeks. It seemed forever as I watched the seasons literally change outside my hospital window from winter to spring. I couldn't wait to get home. On the afternoon of being discharged, my father picked me up at the hospital and, walking into the house, somewhat unsteadily on my new crutches, I caught smells of roast beef and Yorkshire pudding. In that instant, I realized that my mother had cooked my favorite meal to welcome me home. I was overwhelmed with a feeling of being loved and loving her too. Within minutes, however, my mood was shattered. My mother was so drunk that she could barely navigate herself downstairs to greet me. I wanted to escape. I wanted to go back to the hospital. My disappointment was crushing.

Refuge

One of my mother's best friends lived down the street. I liked her a lot and I would often go to her house for tea after school. We never talked about what was going on at home in terms of my mother's drinking, but I knew she knew. I was just relieved and grateful to have her as a safe refuge. She always asked me to wrap all of her Christmas presents and I remember she had beautiful silver paper and thick red and green velvet ribbons. I don't know if I realized how important this woman was during the years of my mother's excessive drinking.

Last Words

There were a couple of days in the last week of June when we didn't have to go to school. I was nearing the end of grade ten and had a couple of days off until the day everyone had to go to pick up report cards. I was going on a picnic with a friend and her mother and had been told to bring my own sandwich. My mother was making it for me that morning and I asked her to "hurry up." Had she been drinking, I would have made my own sandwich, but she'd been sober for a while and I was simply impatient.

I got home late that night when everyone was asleep. The next morning, sometime after my father had gone to work, I went into my mother's room and found her in bed, looking asleep but with her eyes open. It took a few minutes for my brain to compute the reality before my eyes and admit my mother was dead. In among all the reactions I had to this sudden change in my life was enormous guilt that my last words to my mother, the day before, had been a thoughtless order rather than some reflection of love or appreciation that she was trying to stay sober.

She'd been to psychiatrists, she'd been to AA, she'd been in and out of hospitals, she'd had weeks here and there of being sober, but she didn't seem happy, I was impatient, and then she died. I was never told the cause of her death—whether it was intentional or accidental or "normal." All I knew was that she had died, that we didn't talk about it, and no one knew how guilty I felt.

P I face my dad, holding his legs at the knees. I try to believe that my hands have the girth and the power to hold him down if anything should go wrong, but I'm not sure. He thinks it will be OK, though. He sits backwards on the windowsill straining upward out the open window, toward the storm window fastening that has come undone. We are two stories up, in my brother's bedroom.

Nonna, the other grandmother, the one we don't like nearly as well as Poppy, is coming for Christmas. The window in my brother's room, where she will stay during her visit, has rattled for weeks—an annoyance—but now the hardware has become detached in one corner, the hook dangling outside its metal slot, a potential danger to anyone walking below, and a noisy annoyance when the wind blows.

In my memory, my brother is absorbed in a book, ignoring us. It seems to have fallen to me to be the aide-de-camp: sturdy, responsible, ever helpful. My sister, three and a half years younger, is ready for bed, playing with her collection of stuffed animals in the room we share. Mom is at a meeting.

I push down on Dad's legs with all my strength, trying to anchor him to the windowsill. The brown serge fabric of his pants is slippery. I like the color. When he is dressed for work, wearing these same chocolate-colored pants with a tweed sports coat, his broad-brimmed fedora and trench coat, he looks like a movie star. He is probably the most handsome salesman in the world, I think.

We had been roughhousing in the living room. While we were playing, somehow an ice cube from his drink had become involved. Later I would remember that the last thing that happened before we came upstairs was that I'd stolen an ice cube from his drink and put it in his pants. Just after that, the rattling of the storm window drew us upstairs to investigate. I will blame myself for years afterward. I will think he somehow sat on the ice cube and slipped.

The effort to hitch the detached window back onto its hook is not going well. He's having trouble boosting the frame upward using only one hand. The tips of his fingers go white and flat with pressure on the inside molding as he holds himself inside. *One lift of the storm window with both hands at once,* he may have thought . . . *just one moment of balance with my daughter holding my legs, keeping me safe, and the damn window will be back on its hardware, rattle-free, ready for Mom's visit . . .* or perhaps he didn't even think. He let go with his inside hand and lifted the detached window upward with both hands.

Later, I never asked what he had been thinking, or if I did, he never answered. Now, confronted by a height perception, I want to fall to the ground and become part of it to keep myself safe. Looking out over the Grand Canyon or at Manhattan from the Empire State Building causes my knees to buckle and my eyes to well with tears as I see only my father spinning through black space, a helpless figure illuminated against the dark night, slowly spinning downward, beyond help.

He somersaults backwards as he falls. The fall and impact of hitting ground are a moment in time and a sound all at once: a deep metallic thud, overlaid with the tinkling of breaking glass as flesh and bone meet the iron grate covering the basement window well.

I kneel beside him on the cold stone border of the well. How did I get downstairs and outside? Fly? A rapid dripping sound. It must be raining. *No,* it's blood from his head falling onto the frozen leaves at the base of the window well. I notice that the leaves are bordered with designs in frost.

Upstairs fast to get a blanket. Cover a person in shock. Tell my brother to call an ambulance.

Oh no, he's getting up, he's on his knees, his body an inverted "v" under the blanket as he struggles to right himself. He staggers as I run to support him—my 112 pounds against his 220, my 5'5" against his 6'2". We lurch along the stone path of the side yard, the dark and damp yard where there is no sun in the summer. The side yard where we hang the hammock in the shade to escape the Ohio heat . . . the north side, the weather side, where the wind beats against the walls in winter, loosening the storm windows from their fastenings.

Up the steps, through the front door. Blood dripping onto the gold living room rug. We approach ourselves in the mirror that covers the entire wall behind the sofa. My sister and I like to admire ourselves in it as we bounce about in layers of petticoats being ballerinas. But now the mirror reflects a grim vision: a head-injured man draped in a blood-soaked pale-green wool blanket supported by a ponytailed, gawky girl-child in a plaid wool skirt, bloodstained white blouse, kneesocks. We stagger to the couch where he falls, miraculously, on the blanket, *which is good*, I think, *because now the blood won't stain the new gold and rose and teal floral-striped slipcover.*

I run upstairs to the back room, our TV room, for the afghan that lies over the arm of the upstairs couch.

On my return to the stairway I meet my sister, blonde and rosy, in her pale-yellow fuzzy sleeper. "What's the matter?" her voice quavers as she senses certain urgency.

"Dad's hurt. Go to bed." I run down the stairs. A familiar high wail follows me. I turn, frustrated at the distraction: "This is no time for crying. Dad's hurt and I'm taking care of him, so just go to your room. This is not a time for crying."

Oh no! He's getting up again! Running to the couch, I push him back down as forcefully as I can. We struggle. He's fending off my attempts to calm him, telling me to leave him alone. He's fine, he says. He wants to get up. He's just cut his head, he says. He's angry. He overpowers me and stands.

Streaks of dried blood form blotchy forelocks in front of his ears. An eyebrow oozes a ruby glob of gore. The back of his head is matted and running. I can't tell what is hair, what is blood, what may be something from the inside of his head. Everything on the back of his head is red and wet, very wet. There is some white showing. Bone? I get him to sit back down.

My brother stands in the archway between the living room and the entry hall. *Is he just watching?* "I'm going to stand out front and signal for the ambulance," he says, holding up a flashlight. "You call Mom."

The number is written on a white square of notepaper in blue fountain pen in her impossibly even, perfectly slanted handwriting. The paper glows, a beacon of comfort.

I dial. The ring is answered after five peals. I can hear the sound of the group of women in the background. "Hi Mrs. Frederick, this is Polly. May I speak to my mom for a moment please?"

Don't alarm people. Keep calm. Don't create panic.

I wait, then I can hear my mother's deep, melodic voice grow louder as she approaches the phone, still chatting to someone in the room behind her. At last, in my ear, full of smoke, a highball, and the company of other sociable housewives, "Hello."

"Mom, I don't want to worry you, but I have something bad to tell you. Dad just fell out a window."

A flurry of questions: "What? How? When? Which window? Have you called an ambulance? Good girl. I'll be right home," and she's gone. The silence on the other end of the line is a soft, dark place I would like to stay.

But my father is in the living room, injured; my brother outside signaling with the light. Running back to the living room, through the hallway, I pass the stairway to the second floor and can hear my sister, in the bedroom we share, still crying loudly.

My father lurches through the living room archway into the hall, almost colliding with me. He is pale, bedecked with blood, angry now, voice raised, his arms flailing away any attempt to guide him back to the sofa. We argue. He wants to go outdoors. I try to hold the door closed. *If he falls, if he falls down the steps . . .*

He gets past me, opens the door, calls to my brother, "What the hell are you doing?" My brother moves across the frozen grass of the front yard, slowly sweeping the beam of the flashlight into the street in front of the house. *It may help. It may speed the ambulance. Who knows?*

"Help," I call out. "Help me. Dad won't lie down. He wants to come out." My brother approaches the door, I take the flashlight from him. "You try, I can't do it," I cry. "I'll stay out here."

Alone in the yard on the familiar slope of grass, shivering in my thin cotton blouse, I play the beam of light first one way then the other, hoping "They," whoever "*They*" are—policemen, firemen, ambulance drivers . . . adults—will be drawn to the narrow white beam of light. *Where are they? My dad's hurt. I did it. It's my fault. Where are they?*

44

At last an ambulance turns into the driveway. I run for it. Two attendants unload a stretcher, then walk—*Please run, please hurry!*—to the door. My brother opens it. My father lurches up from the couch to greet them. The tall black man strides across the room and puts his hand on my father's chest. "Stay down, pal," he says.

"The hell I will. Who are you anyway? Who called you? I don't need you. I don't need any help."

My mother arrives. Between them, she and the ambulance attendants maneuver my father onto the stretcher, where he is belted down, then carried to and inserted into the back door of the vehicle. My mother is helped into the back of the wagon. Before the door is closed, does she say, "Go to bed kids"? Who stays with us that long night? No one in my memory, although my sister remembers a neighbor being with us.

Much later, they return home. My father's head is bound in bandage. He has forty-eight stitches in the back of his head. Other stitches close smaller cuts over his eyebrow and on his cheek. Mom says the X-rays revealed no breaks. Miraculous. He is to stay in bed and rest.

The next day it is my job to help my father out of bed so that he can walk the few steps to the bathroom. He says he is so stiff he can't raise himself into the sitting position. He offers me both hands and I pull as hard as I can until he is sitting. Then I pull again so that he can stand, then swing myself under his arm to support him. His face beads with sweat as he tries to balance himself over the toilet bowl. I must continue to support him until he relieves himself.

We repeat the pulling in reverse so that he can ease himself onto the bed. The effort leaves him pale and breathless. I have stayed home from school to help. I am in the seventh grade. What is my mother doing, in this memory? I don't know. She is nowhere to be seen in my memory of the room. Just me, and Dad needing my help.

I am keeping watch after dinner from the floral rocking armchair next to my mother's dressing table. My father is sleeping fitfully. We have given up on walking to the bathroom. It is my job to bring the glass milk bottle from the bathroom when he needs it, and to help him position himself to urinate into it, then empty it, and wait again. He wakes and mumbles something unintelligible. I walk to him, then lean forward to hear better.

"The walls," he says in a frightened whisper, "the walls are full of mice. See them?"

"No, Dad, the walls are OK," I say.

"Look, look up there, in that crack, see them?"

"There's no crack, Dad. There aren't any mice."

Visions follow. He describes creatures and scenes so exciting, frightening, and exotic I dare not leave the room for a pen and paper, but instead pull shirt cardboard out of his freshly laundered shirts in the dresser and use my mother's eyebrow pencils to record the apparitions: images by turn horrifying or funny, but all so clear and vivid that I am certain I'm witnessing a sacred moment of delirium, tapping directly into some cosmic truth through a mind stimulated by shock and damage.

Beautiful in its awesome raw power, this is not my father speaking; it is some dark poetic force I do not understand, but know, instinctively is beyond the mortal. I tell myself that this will be important to me as a writer when I grow up. Language and concepts beyond the obvious. Mythical.

I think of my revelation the previous summer as I read *The Odyssey*, peering into a world of adventure that was more interesting than anything I had yet experienced, but familiar, comforting somehow. That's when I realized I wanted to be a writer and knew that I would have to take risks, put myself in dangerous places, experience everything I could so that I would have something to write about. And here it was, in front of me. *Material for writing.* Myth, magic, and terror pour from my father's mouth faster than I can write. I sit and listen and watch.

Two days later he is readmitted to the hospital. Further X-rays reveal several fractured vertebrae. Holes are drilled in his head, he is put into traction. He is operated upon, a tracheotomy performed, wire used to bind bone to bone. Surely it is a miracle that he hadn't died, that I hadn't pulled him to his death trying to raise him to get into the bathroom.

He comes home weeks later in a body cast—a plaster vest reaching from hipbone to the top of his head to keep his upper torso and neck immobilized. Now my job is to reach in through the armholes with a Chinese back scratcher. There are no further visions. Men come, drink, talk in loud voices. The living room is the center of his existence. He sleeps there, eats there. He can't climb the stairs to the bedroom. The room is adrift with smoke.

It is only dozens of years later that I realize that his "visions" had been delirium tremens from alcohol withdrawal, and even more years pass before I learn that the DTs themselves, with their accompanying biochemical shocks, could have killed him.

—∞—

He was a pathetic sight. Slouched in the corner of an expensive sofa, the buttons of his white oxford shirt popping open to reveal his bloated belly. But through the eyes of a nine-year-old child, pathetic was way beyond her reach. This man, her father, was frightening. While the routine was the same every night, the emotional atmosphere was consistent only in its unpredictability. Oblivious to the six-thirty news, the blaring voice of the commentator represented a semblance of a different reality; a reminder that there was a world beyond his soggy existence.

"Pour me another one, sweetie."

Maybe he wouldn't notice if she didn't put so much scotch in this time. Maybe those protruding, yellow eyes which clashed with his overly flushed face would close. Maybe he would die . . .

Please, God, keep me safe.

My Paradox

As a child I was caught in the paradox between what I assumed was normal family dynamics and "something isn't right here." I really didn't understand the effects of alcohol on our family until after my mother died when I was eight years old. I always assumed that my father's drinking was a direct result of the horrible car accident that killed not only her, but also one of my brothers, my mother's best friend, and three of her children. Our family was devastated, and I thought he drank because his grief was so unbearable.

It was and he did, but what I began to understand later, after years of family stories, was that my dad was an alcoholic when he married my mother. In fact, it seems she had gone to Florida with her best friend, her best friend's children, and my three brothers to figure things out. (My baby sister was too young to go on the trip and I was on a trip to Hawaii with my grandparents.) After fighting with my father on the phone because she wanted to stay away longer, my mother was killed on the way home. Her decision was made for her and our family was completely shattered.

I was the oldest of five children and while I don't remember much before my mother's death, I do believe that, as a young child, I was witness to a lot of fighting and drunken behavior. My memories are clearer after the accident and I was witness to incredible and unending chaos rooted in profound sadness.

My three remaining siblings and I never spoke about the alcohol abuse until years had passed. Initially we didn't talk because we were so young and were simply trying to find ways to adapt and survive. And later, we still didn't talk because all three of my siblings were beginning their own downward spirals into substance abuse and I essentially left home when I was sent to boarding school at the age of thirteen.

Moments of Light

In the midst of the madness, there were certainly moments of light. Thankfully, I have happy memories of playing with my brothers and new baby sister, living in a wonderful house, and being well cared for by a variety of loving "help."

I did sense that my father loved me to the best of his limited emotional capacity, and I do remember his wonderful sense of humor despite all the pain. And my grandmother, who had lost her beloved daughter when my mother died, loved me desperately. In many ways it was not a healthy love in that she used me to replace my mother in her life. Still, spending time with her, though not always safe because she was also an alcoholic, did provide a place of refuge for which I will always be thankful.

Treading Carefully

I am all grown up now, but under this capable adult dwells a fearful, angry child healing, but treading carefully and very slowly.

You see . . . for me it is no longer about the sordid details of my dysfunctional past. The significance of the chronological events has dimmed. Instead the focus has shifted from my head to my heart. My healing journey began by labeling myself as an ACOA and acknowledging my own dysfunction. To move beyond the label, however, and truly break the cycle, past events had to become the key to unlocking my feeling memories. My intellect enabled the over-adaptive behavior which helped me to survive as a child, but as my life unfolded these behaviors began to backfire. I had a husband, three healthy children, and lots of friends, but I was dying inside. Something was desperately wrong . . . something essential was missing.

—⁘—

When we first shared these original writings with each other, our reactions were the same: "Although I thought I knew you really well, I had no idea what you had gone through." We were struck by what had emerged through these first writings—images, details, emotions, context. We could literally see, through the written words, how we shared a number of feelings from our childhood experiences. Our understanding of and empathy toward each other was deepened.

We became even more convinced that we should write more and try to put together a collection of our memories. We wanted to explore further and go deeper. Our next step was to go away for a weekend during which we generated a list of loaded words to serve as prompts for spontaneous writing.

—ɯ—

We can't return to our childhood and ask
that it be different. We need to learn how to
accept, nurture, and fulfill ourselves.

—Tara Brach

Chapter 4

The List: Our Loaded Words

Writing is a very sturdy ladder out of the pit.
—Louise DeSalvo

The Complete List

Our list of loaded words emerged from a brainstorming conversation at our first gathering. The question had been, "What words spark memories for you?"

This is certainly not an exhaustive list of words that we could have generated. However, we all agreed to stop when someone simply said, "I think we have enough to begin."

We explored the concept of spontaneous writing with the word "hope" and were impressed with what was created from nothing in as short a time as ten minutes. Something as simple as picking a word and writing spontaneously intrigued us enough to choose more words.

The words in bold (including "hope") are the words we chose as prompts for our spontaneous writing exercises. Clearly, many of the other words are also suitable for writing exercises in their own right.

We picked fourteen words and then we chose to stop. We could have chosen thirteen or fifteen or eighteen. There were no rules and so we were free to make our own decisions. You can do so too!

blame	feelings	forgiveness
siblings	**resolution**	understanding
survival	compassion	illusion/reality
fear	accomplishment	**shame**
hope	holidays	empties/cigarettes
sleep	bedtime	middle of the night
destiny	loyalty	parties
laughter/**humor**	naked	funerals/death
abandonment	confusion	vulnerability
love/hate	other parent	safety/danger
community/home	role reversal	**badge of courage/ membership**
loneliness	paranoia	physical self
anger	**unpredictability**	sounds and smells
money	relationships	peacemakers
spirituality	strength	control
creativity	manipulation	responsibility
letting go	courage	knowing/feeling
chasing/running	guilt	**gifts**
accountability	blame	warrior
Christmas	compensation	denial
surrender	**neglect**	secrets
lies	excuses	vigilance/ hypervigilance

The Words We Chose

For each word we used to spark spontaneous writing, we have included a dictionary definition as well as some commentary about the significance of the word/term for children of alcoholics. It should be noted that the definitions and commentaries were created for this book, long after our writing had taken place, and so did not influence our spontaneous writings.

Even with the words we chose, sometimes only one or two people were inspired enough to write something and sometimes words were blended together (e.g., badge of courage/membership and community/home).

Writing in response to each of these fourteen words was typically done spontaneously, in a limited period of time, and several offerings are very short. In other cases, the words kept flowing and longer pieces were created. Some words inspired short stories; other words triggered only frustration. Sometimes short poems emerged and, in one case, an alternative version of the Lord's Prayer was created.

Remember, we didn't have any rules—just each other's encouragement to try to write for at least ten minutes. The words presented opportunities to just take out the plug and see what flowed.

Your Words?

What words spark memories for you? What words would you want to add? Can you come up with your own list of loaded words unique to your individual circumstances? This might be a good time to make some notes!

Are you inclined to try writing in response to one of these words right now? All you need to do is close your eyes and put your finger down on the paper and then write about the word you landed on for ten to twenty minutes. Don't like the word your finger hit? Oh well—try writing anyway. You might surprise yourself.

But don't be too hard on yourself if you pick a word and nothing comes. Not every word works as a prompt, or may not work on a given day. If this happens, don't conclude, "I'm not a writer!" Try again tomorrow . . . or come up with your own word that sparks something for you.

For now, explore the various offerings that follow . . . hopefully they will strike chords of familiarity, inspire you to try your own writing, or, at the very least, take you more deeply into our worlds.

What is not ex-pressed is de-pressed.

—Mark Nepo

Abandonment

- to have protection, support, or help withdrawn; to be forsaken utterly

- a sense of loss, being left, forgotten, minimized, betrayed

---

The word "abandonment" means more than the obvious image of being left alone or left somewhere, to fend for oneself. One can feel abandoned, at least emotionally so, in a room with family members. People who work with children of alcoholics typically say that abandonment and shame are two of the most significant traits of a dysfunctional home.

When one has been abandoned, literally or figuratively, as shown in the writing samples here, it becomes very difficult for abandoned ones to trust the future or to trust love. When one has been abandoned emotionally—having rarely or never been told that one has done well or that one is loved—a natural consequence can be growing into adulthood doubting that one is ever good enough, is loveable, or is worthy of love.

These deep feelings can continue to raise their ugly heads for years. Feelings of abandonment, not being good enough, can morph into becoming an overachiever; trying to control one's circumstances; clinging to others; always asking "Do you love me?" when in the throes of falling in love, or even when married, and rarely trusting an affirmative answer.

The legacies of abandonment are tenacious and last for years unless addressed.

PFor me, the word "abandonment" brings up memories about the feeling of being left out as well as being left.

When I was a younger adult I tried never to expect anything because nothing could be expected. Or, I would try to anticipate the worst in any situation, because then, at least, once I *had* been disappointed by any situation, at least I had not expected more. I guess I am speaking here of the sort of emotional abandonment that comes from not having the opportunity to process emotions. Process emotions! How about simply being permitted to feel them and to express the feeling of them? Well, I guess that leads into another topic entirely which maybe we'll uncover when I write about other loaded words.

Going back to the idea of expectations, I *so* wanted things to be as they could be but never would be. Abandonment sounds so linear, but it isn't, because it affects so many things around it. The word "abandonment" seems more web-shaped than linear to me.

When I was younger I didn't realize the experiences I was having would later be understood in terms such as "abuse" or "abandonment." The situations I was in were simply my life and certainly didn't feel like any of these loaded words I am now considering. Later, however, I began to understand that words are not unequivocal, that terms carry meaning for individuals and do not necessarily describe just one situation or another, just one case or another. For example, I didn't know that I'd been "abandoned" by my father through his illness of alcoholism, but, here's a story illustrating how feelings I didn't know I had could be triggered by something like a holiday. I'll title my story "Happy Father's Day," but really, the theme is abandonment.

Happy Father's Day

My neighbor came across the street and knocked on the door. I joined her on my front porch. She liked to talk, and I wasn't in a particular mood for conversation, it being Father's Day and me being alone again on one of the "greeting card holidays."

"It's Father's Day," she said. "My kids are at their dad's. I just thought I'd see what you were up to."

"My kid's at his dad's too," I said, adding, "I hate Father's Day." I knew her father had been an alcoholic, disconnected, a general disappointment. And, like me, she had been long divorced, so Father's Day was no occasion for celebration for her either.

"I hate it too," she said. I could see that her eyes were beginning to well with tears as she admitted why she was really standing at my door.

"Our dads didn't do what fathers are supposed to," I said, my throat tightening around the words. I could feel tears welling in my own eyes, but I don't cry easily or readily, especially not on my front porch in front of a neighbor. I'd never been conscious of it, but Father's Day was bringing up enormous feelings of abandonment. *I will have to think about that*, I told myself.

"I never had a dad I could thank for anything." My dad was a failure as a protector and a provider, I felt. Despite my best efforts to keep things on a rational, conversational level, a tear escaped and ran down my face. I rather hoped she wouldn't notice. But she did, and moved to wrap me in a big hug. I was embarrassed, but it felt good to have her arms around me.

"We hate Father's Day," she said, crying and holding me.

"We hate Father's Day," I agreed, softly. She began to sob.

In that moment, I felt understood, acknowledged. The feeling was so unfamiliar as to be almost unbearable. Grief ripped itself from where I'd buried it somewhere very deep in my body and rose in my chest until it couldn't be contained. A sob escaped me. Then another.

We both cried until the tears abated, then held each other at arm's length and said in unison, almost as though we'd rehearsed it, *"We hate Father's Day!"*

Then, standing on my front porch, in full view of the entire neighborhood, we held each other and cried again, and we cried until we just had to laugh. It was a new kind of happy on Father's Day.

—⟶⟵—

H When I was sent to boarding school at the age of thirteen, I felt relieved to get out of the insanity of my house but also felt abandoned by my family. My father had remarried six months after my mother's death and our family system was in complete turmoil for the next eight years. Constant fighting and endless drinking created an environment of emotional neglect and fear.

It took me years to uncover that at the root of all my fears was the belief that anyone I loved would leave me . . . now or then . . . sooner or later . . . through death or simply by not being available to me physically, emotionally, or spiritually. Truth be told, that felt like my experience through much of my life, and that fear has prevented me from opening my heart and soul completely to those who I do love and who love me . . . my husband, children, friends, myself, my god. But as I have journeyed, as I have attempted to acknowledge and to embrace that fear, I have gradually opened my heart and shared my soul a little more, and a little more, and then a little more.

It is a huge risk for me to fully love someone and to trust that they won't abandon me intentionally. It is also a big accomplishment each time I do take that risk and remind myself that there will always be someone who will not abandon me.

—m—

Badge of Courage/Membership

- badge: a special distinctive mark, token, or device
- courage: quality of mind or spirit that enables a person to face difficulty, danger, pain
- membership: the state of belonging to or being part of a group

Does it take courage to be a child of an alcoholic? Does it take courage to find ways to negotiate the landscape of childhood without the helpful fuel of emotional support? Does it take courage to admit that things in your home do not match the images on happy greeting cards? Does it take courage to say, to another person, "My parent is an alcoholic"?

Children of alcoholics, as children, have no idea whether they are being courageous or not . . . they just know what they know, even if what is "normal" for them is dysfunctional. And when these children are praised for "coping well," for "being strong," for "being brave," sometimes a child's reaction is only to be reminded that they wish they didn't have to cope, be strong, or be brave. Sometimes they would prefer not to have a badge.

Membership is typically something that one chooses, like a club someone decides to join. However, the membership of being a child of an alcoholic is imposed. Whether memberships are chosen or imposed, there is still the option of being an active or inactive member.

Children of alcoholics who are "inactive" tend to keep their membership secret, while "active" members seek to declare their membership and benefit from being with other active members. One way of being active is through groups such as Alateen (for teenagers), Al-Anon and/or the Adult Children of Alcoholics (ACA or ACOA) fellowship (for adults), or Al-Anon Family Groups (which include young children). Each of these groups offers Twelve Step meetings and resources to support recovery from the legacies of a dysfunctional childhood. The primary purpose of these groups, which honor anonymity, is to create a safe setting in which young adults and adults can share their stories, strength, and hope with others in a meaningful manner.

It is in such groups, as it was in our little group, that courage can arise through choosing to be honest, forthright, and gentle with oneself.

LWhen I was a teenager, three of us, two friends both named Mary and I, had this special badge. It wasn't like a Brownie badge—you know, the kind you'd get for making your bed for three weeks or writing a pen pal in Peru, the kind you'd wear with pride on your sleeve. We weren't proud of our badge. It was for a secret society. As far as we knew, there weren't any other members. The badge said, "My mother is an alcoholic."

We each had one of these badges but we wouldn't wear them. Actually, that's not exactly true. Sometimes we'd put them on if we were visiting each other, sitting on our beds cross-legged or with our feet tucked underneath, gabbing about dumb teachers or giggling about boys or pouring over a stack of romance comics or listening to Elvis. These were moments of comfort, moments when you could forget your life on the other side of the door, moments when you didn't have to explain why your mother was lying on the floor when you got home from school, moments when you didn't have to die of embarrassment because your mother couldn't speak without slurring her words. We'd all been through the initiation rites of this secret society and so just knew things without having to say them. So it didn't matter if we wore the badges or not—we just quietly knew each other could see the badges whether we wore them or not.

We'd certainly never wear our badges outside of the house. No one was to know about our secret, private worlds. Most people just thought we were ordinary teenagers. We got involved in everything we could at school. We played on all the teams, we participated in student council activities, we were members of the school orchestra and choir. If we could excel and be very good at something, this is what we'd do. Otherwise, we tried very hard to just blend in and find good reasons for not going home.

As time passed and we got older, the significance of our secret society and our badges changed. Away from home and out in the world, we began to get inklings that there were more members than we realized. But more often than not, at least initially, we wouldn't publicly admit to being a member. The badges stayed tucked inside the chambers of our hearts.

And then, with one person at a time, within the envelope of friendship, we would carefully inch out the edges of our badges. If it felt safe, we would bring the whole badge out. With those we discovered as mutual members of this secret society, sharing our badges often was the focus of our attention. We understood each of us bore scars but did not take the time to look at them in detail. The badge was enough, a symbol for emotional short-hand, a shortcut to empathy, no-questions-asked automatic bonding.

Of course, if the other person to whom we were opening our hearts and showing our badge was not a member, we would have to explain what having the badge meant, what the demands were to earn it, why we'd kept it a secret. In those initial moments of disclosure, it often felt as though we were naked and the badge was not big enough to cover our scars or our shame. But, more often than not, the response from friends was one of wonder, admiration, and a deepened level of respect. They saw us as brave, strong, and resilient survivors.

Over time, we began to think of our badges as badges of courage. Rather than feeling ashamed of our past, we started to wear our badges to explain ourselves. Like soldiers, we were saying, "Look. See. I was in a war. I'm a hero. It's not my fault I am the way I am. It was the war. My badge proves it." We had traveled the road from shame to pride. It felt good. It felt like we had "arrived." It was a better place than where we'd hidden our experiences and kept our hearts closed.

But the journey was not, is not, over. Just as some soldiers get to the point where they want to be seen and understood for more than their medals and war records, some of us too want to move past our badges and stories of what has been.

Life is about more than what we've been through. It is also about what we can be with what we've learned. It's about not repeating the patterns of denial we've learned so well. It's about acknowledging needs and learning to ask for help. It's about developing trust. It's about not assuming responsibility for others. It's about learning to take emotional risks.

If we choose to continue to wear our badges on our sleeves, even though they are badges of courage, it is likely the full potential of our hearts will not be seen, understood, or felt. Like soldiers who choose to see their experiences around war and death and destruction in the context of peace, we too can choose to see our experiences around alcoholism and abandonment and fear in the context of the possibility of love.

— ❧ —

Por me the phrase "Badge of Courage" means "membership."

"You too?" asked Liz all those years ago. "You too?"

This condition of being a grown woman who grew up with alcoholic parents is a membership, especially for women "of an age," such as myself.

When I was growing up, the prevalent idea was that women were in service, not only to men but also to all others. The female role created a sorority of caretakers—a kind of undeclared society wherein each of us developed roles and rituals—controlling, organizing, explaining, understanding, smoothing, taking care of, looking outward at others to serve instead of inward at ourselves in order to develop. Years later—once the shame and secrecy of growing up in an alcoholic family had lessened/dissolved, once it could be admitted, that "yes, my father was a desperate alcoholic"—a mutual understanding between us female children of alcoholics was created about what characteristics we might share, along with an unspoken clarity about what the emotional experience had been.

One of the hardest things for me growing up was not feeling membership anywhere because of my secret about Dad's alcoholic sickness. One of the best things about adulthood for me has been to have felt affiliations—a sense of belonging to certain groups through experiences that have similarities.

When I was a child, the membership in the group "children of alcoholics" was unknown to me since no one spoke of such things. Even into adulthood, unless it came up in some unlikely context, this membership was covert, and if there were an occasion when the membership happened to be mentioned, the "You too?" response might be the end of the conversation. Until I became involved in this loaded words project, I kept quiet about the membership.

Keeping quiet isn't easy, though. Asked if my parents are still living, my answer has to be, "My mother is still alive and healthy." The following question invariably is, "Oh? When did your father die?" to which my invariable answer is, "Quite a while ago . . . I guess I must have been about twenty-eight."

Then might come The Question, the one I don't want to answer—"He must have died young. Was he ill?"—to which I

67

give a variety of answers, such as, "Yes, he died of pneumonia." This is, in fact, true but is only part of the story, being simply the immediate cause of death. My truth, however, is that he died as a direct result of his addiction to cigarettes—that is, nicotine—and, just a little less obviously, from the illness of alcohol addiction.

Sometimes the membership card—my Badge of Courage—is elicited through an innocent question such as, "What did your father do for work?" The half-truth, easy-way-out answer is, "He was a salesman; he sold cardboard boxes." The truth is, "He didn't work during the last dozen years of his life. He was a serious alcoholic." Then comes, often, "You too?"

Understanding the importance of this membership saved my life, I'd say. In Adult Children of Alcoholics (ACOA) Twelve Step meetings, I would hear others forgive themselves for their shortcomings—even excuse their parents' shortcomings and abuses with the words, "They were doing the best they could." This allowed me to begin to forgive myself for my own shortcomings.

I was doing the best I could, too, had always been doing the best I could under the circumstances even though, before gaining perspective through these Al-Anon–sponsored ACOA meetings, I had attempted perfection, which is the enemy of "doing your best."

Now, though, if I allowed myself to truly believe that under the circumstances I was "doing my best," then this membership became a solace, a place of tender mercies. In this place, where neither I nor anyone else could expect perfection, I could return to console and forgive myself. Here I could reidentify my strengths and weaknesses based on my membership identity and could gain consolation for the ways in which my distrust of the world (for example fear of self-revelation) might be understood—and hopefully, worked on—in the larger context of "adult child of an alcoholic."

Tomorrow's strength is gained from suffering today. As a child, some defenses become anti-interactive, negative strengths—such as the walls one builds for self-protection. Some results of suffering as a child are positive: a deep understanding of human nature and paradoxical relationships; a tolerance for not knowing; an ability to organize even the most hopelessly muddled information into a systematically ordered "best possible" order.

One can't resign this membership—adult child of an alcoholic—but one can become resigned to it. Years of examination can turn to a more comfortable lived-in feeling of "oh, yes, that . . . yes, it did affect me, and now it has become a lapel pin, a 'badge of courage.'" Yes, I suppose so. All the valiant children. And I was one of them.

There are even more senses of membership for me involving alcohol: the membership with others who are survivors of family disasters; membership with those who come to realize that their family-of-origin issues created conspiracies of secrecy, cover-ups, and lies many families use to hide their less desirable attributes; and, overall, the membership of belonging with any fellow sufferer as we all, after all, are.

—⚊—

Hometimes I think I have "PILLAR OF STRENGTH" tattooed on my forehead! Honest to God . . . there was a period in my life where if one more person told me how strong I was . . . how I was this tower of strength who sustained what felt like the entire universe . . . I wanted to punch them and then throw up.

There is no doubt that I still come across as strong, capable, confident, responsible (puke), assertive, resilient, practical (barf),

69

reasonable . . . the classic hero (how fucking tiring)!! Fortunately after years of therapy, I have come to appreciate that some of those words do still apply to me, but hopefully in a healthier way. And, the cost to me is not so high because, in time, I finally began to allow my vulnerability to shine through.

—⁂—

Community/Home

- the place where one lives, where one's domestic affections are centered
- any group sharing common characteristics or interests
- any place of residence or refuge

By all outward appearances, we three grew up in homes located in relatively affluent communities; to an outsider, it might well have looked as though we had everything going for us. However, the words "home" and "community" mean so much more than physical structures and neighborhoods. All three of us struggled to find love and meaning under our roofs of origin. Clearly, unless we know people's stories, we never really know what goes on behind the doors of a "home."

One of the most common attributes in homes where alcohol abuse is present is a code of silence, the proverbial "elephant in the room" that no one talks about. Therefore, based on the definitions above, key words jump out as often being absent for children of alcoholics: "domestic affections are centered"; "sharing"; "refuge."

Because of the holes in one's sense of home and community, some children of alcoholics go out of their way to try to ensure, when they become parents themselves, that their children will experience a healthy and fulsome sense of home and community. While this desire comes from the best of intentions, it can be a manifestation of a child of an alcoholic's desire to try to be perfect. Trying to be perfect is exhausting, and there is no such thing.

I have lived
in dwellings
all over the world
Sometimes for
only one night and
sometimes for
years on end
Houses, apartments,
other people's homes.
Hotels, ships, trains
Even under the stars of a Japanese sky
But a dwelling is not
necessarily
a home
A dwelling
is only a stopping place . . .
a home
speaks of roots, safety, love
I have homes
to go to all over the world . . .
friends
I have shared
a home
with my chosen family
And I have learned
that I always
have a home
within myself
But as a child
I do not recall
having a home

—⚏—

Chapter 4 ◆ *The List: Our Loaded Words*

LWhen I was a teenager, and even into my early twenties, I gave serious consideration to becoming Jewish. Among other books I read around that time was Sammy Davis Jr.'s autobiography, *Yes I Can!* I figured, "If he can do it, so can I!"

The more I considered this possibility, though, the more I realized that what I really wanted was not the religious aspect of being Jewish but, rather, the sense of belonging. To be able to say "I'm Jewish" would associate me with people who had a history, who shared the bonds of persecution, who were part of a community.

And eventually I concluded that I could not get to this notion of "community" via religion. I could not especially put on the cloak of Judaism and claim the clothing to also be my history and culture. I felt it would be insincere and wrong to use a religious path to get to a place that had nothing to do with faith. I would have to find community elsewhere.

And I have.

I have found community with people who share interests, values, principles.

I belong to a community of readers . . . in my book club and in any bookstore, anywhere in the world.

I belong to a community of adults who believe children benefit from care and love.

I belong to a community of Canadians who cry when the national anthem is spontaneously sung.

I belong to a community of ordinary folk who think the world can be a better place and that each of us can make a difference in making it better.

I belong to a community of human beings who understand the unconditional love of a dog.

I belong to a community of people who feel humble in the context of the earth and its ecosystem.

And I belong to a community of women who, without words, understand so much.

—〰—

PI don't know where I live, and never have.

I didn't feel at home where I came from, and couldn't wait to leave, which I did at eighteen for college, then again at nineteen for a different college, and then again at twenty for my third college. I finished my third college, but it never became "home."

I married just out of college and moved from Ohio to Vermont, but two months later my husband and I moved to New York, so New England hadn't been home. I had never wanted to live in New York. It certainly wasn't home. After five years there, and graduate school, I found myself divorced and moved to Boston, but that wasn't home either. It was only a way station.

More moves followed. I kept trying to find my place, to get comfortable, to get it right, to "be at home."

After twenty moves in twenty years, on entering Al-Anon, I learned that I had been enacting what Twelve Step programs call the "geographic solution." What finally stopped all the moving was not me coming to my senses, exactly, but my dawning realization that I could not keep moving once my child was of school age. So, not for myself, but for another I could stop enacting the geographic solution and stay still.

But now my child is twenty and I realize that the house I've kept as a home for him is not a home for me. "Home" has meant the relationship I have had with my child: shared time, emotions, concerns, efforts. Home means responsible interactions. Home means predictability.

—∿—

HWhen I think about my experiences as a child this word—"home"—conjures up a lot of opposites . . . aloneness, isolation, separateness, and incredible longing. I would have done just about anything to have created a healthy and nurturing community for myself . . . a sense of a "normal" family. I tried desperately to do just that. Mind you no one would have acknowledged that our family wasn't wonderful, and the last thing I appeared to be was lonely. But I was dying inside.

The community which surrounded me as a child, whether it was family or friends, was sick and distorted. But somewhere in the midst of all the craziness there was a knowing in me. Some instinct which, as I moved into adulthood, led me to places or people where I did feel loved and supported . . . boarding school, the family I created with my husband, a community of wonderfully grounded friends, the church, God. The paradox of course is that, while I love community and seem to constantly seek it out, I also have come to really value my aloneness more and more. What a gift to have a choice to savor both.

—∿—

Fear

- a distressing emotion aroused by impending danger, evil, or pain
- feeling of dread, panic, concern, anxiety, foreboding

For children of alcoholics, fear often is both a specific focus as well as a general state of being. For example, one can be specifically afraid, from past experiences, that when a parent is drunk, his or her anger will come to the fore and there will be yelling and screaming and throwing. But in a more general way, there can be a generalized and permeating all-the-time fear, not knowing what will come next, creating a pervasive sense of anxiety and foreboding.

It is an interesting exercise to have children of alcoholics complete the sentence, "I am afraid of _____." Responses would likely include "being abandoned," "being embarrassed," "being hurt," and "not knowing what is coming next."

When children experience fear, specific or general, where do they typically turn for help or a sense of safety? The answer, of course, is "home." But where does a child turn if the source of fear is within the home? Children of alcoholics, therefore, can also experience the trauma of feeling they have nowhere to turn when they are afraid.

How does a child of an alcoholic cope in the face of such fears? Some remove themselves, either literally, leaving the house, or figuratively, withdrawing into themselves. Some try, in their own ways, to calm the waters, to make peace in the family, to be general people pleasers. It doesn't take too much imagination to see how these coping mechanisms can manifest in adulthood:

"In the face of conflict, just leave."

"When there's trouble, offer a cup of tea but don't talk about what is happening."

"Apologize for everything, even if you are not responsible."

L As a child, I was afraid of the yelling and screaming fights between my parents, afraid that they would become physical and that someone would get hurt. I also carried around the fear that if things didn't get better, my mother was going to be committed to a mental hospital in Montreal that had a terrible reputation. I was terrified that she might have to go to this place where, so stories went, people lived like animals.

But, the most persistent fear I had as a child was the daily, quiet-but-always-there fear about going home after school. As I opened the door each day, I'd wonder where she'd be, whether she'd be drunk, whether she had hurt herself. Arriving home was always filled with anxiety.

As an adult, I will never forget the sensation of my first full-blown anxiety attack. It happened late one night while I was talking to my sister on the phone. I had just started telling her about finding a man at the gym, collapsed, "in extremis," at the point of dying, and how hard it was to breathe while I ran to get help. And, once again, I suddenly could not breathe. I was terrified. I thought I was having a heart attack. I imagined I was going to die. I went to sleep that night wondering if I would wake up in the morning.

Through talking, relaxation exercises, and drops of homeo-pathic "Rescue Remedy," I came to understand my distress emerged from the fact that this discovery of a man with his eyes fully open but lying still, stiff and unresponsive, had catapulted me back twenty-six years in time to the scene in my mother's bed-room where I found her with her eyes fully open but lying still, stiff and unresponsive. While I didn't know it at the moment of finding my mother, I soon learned that my mother was dead.

Even though this scene, with my mother as the centerpiece, has been etched in my brain as a visual and factual image, finding a person near the point of death unearthed an emotional connection, long buried and, possibly, never expressed. Way back then, at that pivotal moment of my childhood, as I waited with my sister for the doctor and the police to arrive, I don't remember feeling afraid. I lost myself in all that was happening and, of course, I was busy "being strong" (or so people said). But there I was, twenty-six years later, experiencing the deep roots of my emotions and memories, confronting fear, grappling with my own mortality.

And like my mother, the man at the gym also died.

—⚍—

P Halfway through my thirty-ninth year, in unacknowledged grief over a flurry of impending abandonments, I decided to move—to move not just from apartment to apartment, but to leave my adopted country where I'd lived for ten years, and to move back to the US. I left everything I had and the many people I'd grown to love because of fear. I feared what would happen to me as many of my current support systems changed. My landlords, who had become family to me and my son, living on the second and third floors while we lived on the first, were talking about moving to a new home and selling the building. Other close friends who lived around the corner were moving away too. My job was ending. A project I was working on was undone and unfunded. My divorce had become final and my former husband had left on an extended trip. Basically, I was leaving so that I would not be left—understandable emotionally, but also, emotionally, a drastic mistake. Six months after moving, I realized the move was the worst thing I could have done.

Having moved and now edging toward forty, I hated myself for failing at marriage. This was, after all, my second time. I hated where I lived, the work I was doing, what I looked like. I hated being lonely. I hated never having enough money. And I *hated-hated-hated* that I was still a smoker, knowing that smoking was a disgusting, stinking, harmful, expensive addiction that I felt inexorably bound to.

I felt weak, powerless, defeated, shot. I felt very sorry for myself, very angry at everyone and everything. Life seemed so empty. I was hopeless. Or was I?

It occurred to me that perhaps if I could gain control of one thing, make one major change, I would feel better about things.

I had always been a person with a cigarette. In fact, I had smoked, beginning at age twelve, because my father drank. Smoking was my way of becoming the adult I felt I had to be because of the "family problem." And smoking had become part of the fabric of my being, a substitute for feelings, for father, for just about anything.

So, in order to do something good for myself at this time when I felt so terrible about everything else, I stopped smoking. It was terribly difficult but I was spurred on by the idea that I had smoked since I was twelve and here I was forty! If I didn't stop soon, I'd be wearing an oxygen mask and my son would have an invalid mom.

So I stopped; but what I hadn't considered was what happens to an addict once the addictive substance is removed. I began to have crying jags. I'd suddenly find my eyes filling up with tears, then spilling over without provocation. I could barely contain my impatience or contempt for others' ineptitude or stupidity. I began waking up at four in the morning unable to go back to sleep.

By the time I went to see a psychiatrist, I was hanging on by a very thin thread. My days were a blur of battling the urge to smoke now accompanied by an even stronger urge to just end the suffering.

I knew I was depressed, knew I needed therapy and probably antidepressant drugs, and asked the psychiatrist to see me as many times as he would require to diagnose me and recommend a course of therapy. He prescribed an antidepressant and explained that it would take three weeks to reach a therapeutic dosage level. Meanwhile, however, he explained, I would begin gradually to feel better.

By the end of our third session I was indeed feeling a bit better. I was not nearly as shaky and my sleep and appetite had been restored.

"I want you to understand something," the psychiatrist said at that final session. "Your father was an alcoholic and you've suffered lasting repercussions from what happened to you as a result. The way for you to get better is to go to Al-Anon–sponsored Adult Children of Alcoholics meetings to find out why you are the way you are and why you began smoking in the first place."

I was furious. This was not the deal we had struck. He was supposed to tell me who to see for therapy. Controlling my anger and a rising feeling of betrayal, I told him I wanted his recommendation of a therapist I could see.

"What you need is Al-Anon," he repeated. He handed me a book about alcoholism called *I'll Quit Tomorrow* and a printed schedule of Al-Anon Adult Children of Alcoholics meetings. "Promise yourself you'll go to at least six meetings before you make a judgment about them," he said. "Take your medicine, go to Al-Anon, and you will get better and stay better."

I went to an Al-Anon meeting. It seemed like the AA meetings you read about. From what I could see, there seemed to be an obvious in-group, people who talked about themselves, taking turns. There was the "anonymous" introduction each time a person spoke—"Hi, my name is Carl"—and the group response: "Hi, Carl." There was a table covered with Al-Anon and AA literature and a raffle from which someone won one of the self-help books on the table. There was also a lot of hugging and an interest in me that didn't seem properly anonymous. I was *not* impressed.

The next week I attended another meeting at the same place. This time what seemed to be the "in-group" had an argument on a point of procedure. One participant rambled on for about twenty minutes, describing difficult circumstances from his past week. A woman, who described herself as an alcoholic, overeater, drug abuser, and child of alcoholics, spoke overlong too. I found the experience unpleasant, but at least the procedures were more familiar than the previous week. The next time I went, the same sorts of things occurred. I could see no benefit to me from this. It was my third and last meeting. *To hell with going to six meetings*, I thought and didn't go back again.

I continued to take my antidepressant pills and began therapy with someone I found on my own. It felt good to begin to explore my past and to talk about the sorts of things that had led to smoking and to stopping smoking. I learned that depression is misplaced anger, an emotion so strong (and for some reason so unacceptable to the person feeling it) that the anger is instead turned against the self.

During my therapy I had come to understand that taking up smoking in the first place had been an act of rebellion spurred by my resentment at having adult responsibilities that began at age eleven due to my father's alcoholism. In my child-mind, I'd concluded, *If I have to act like an adult, I'll take on adult privileges.* Hence, the smoking was deeply connected to old anger.

I felt a messianic zeal to explain smoking to other nicotine addicts in a palatable way so that they might get mad too. Mad enough to quit. I decided to write a book about it.

As luck would have it, I ran into the psychiatrist on the street one day during this period of intense research, writing, and querying. He asked me how I was feeling. *Better, definitely, but not well.* "Are you going to Al-Anon?" he asked. When he heard that I had not made it beyond three meetings, he just smiled.

"You won't feel better until you start going to meetings," he said. "I'm an adult child of alcoholics myself," he continued, "and all the therapy in the world didn't help me until I understood the impact of an alcoholic parent on my life. Go to Al-Anon. Give yourself at least six meetings." He explained, too, that not all groups suited all people, and suggested that I go to a variety of places for meetings at different times of day and night. He said that the AA hotline would be able to tell me where and when meetings were scheduled.

He was right. The next meeting I went to was as different from the first three as day and night. The room was bright and cheerful, the participants Waspy-looking like me, and the program brisk and impersonal. I began to hear things I could identify with. I left the meeting feeling definitely anonymous and definitely buoyed up. It seemed as though somehow these meetings might help me to understand how my own addiction to nicotine might have affected my emotional life and perhaps even how growing up with an alcoholic parent might have affected me in ways I didn't yet understand.

I went to Al-Anon meetings two or three times a week for the next year. I learned to understand my mother better, forgive my father his alcoholism, and to recognize that I was myself a prime candidate for alcoholism if I wasn't careful. I had always given myself time to think, but not to feel. Apparently, I had used a drug, nicotine, to suppress feeling. When I gave up the drug, the feelings, unleashed but not understood, threatened to destroy me. I needed to be alone, vulnerable, and honest with others who had experienced similar things, to learn how to deal with feelings that were very painful, peeling away the veneer of reason to see the emotional suppression below.

The first step it was suggested I take was to admit that, ultimately, I was powerless over other people, or over "things," and that, whether I knew it or not at the time, I always had been. This was the beginning of the "recovery" process that, in Al-Anon, means recovering your sense of personal identity and integrity, rather than always trying to help, guide, control, or manipulate others at what is, ultimately, your own expense.

—⁂—

HI have a deeply entrenched fear that if I am not good enough, or don't try hard enough, or don't control everyone and everything in my life, that I will be abandoned and then I will die. Just when I think I have successfully quieted that fear, it rears its ugly head again and scares the hell out of me! I am so very tired of being driven by this fear . . . this desperate need to control my environment to somehow assure my survival.

This fear is rooted in my "inner child" who struggled so valiantly for emotional survival. I continue to remind myself that, as a forty-three-year-old woman, I no longer need to activate old behaviors when I feel scared, but old habits die hard.

Gifts

- something bestowed or acquired without any particular effort

- inheritance; legacy

The instinct to survive is strong in everyone and children are no different. Children of alcoholics often are high achievers (because they are trying to be perfect); mature for their years (because they had to take on adult tasks while still young); responsible, dependable, and good organizers (because they tried to make order out of chaos); people pleasers (because they wanted to reduce or avoid conflict); good at handling crises (because they probably handled several); and empathetic (because they know that life is often difficult).

While these attributes have their origins in difficulty, they are, for the most part, wonderful strengths that many children of alcoholics take with them into adulthood. The key to honoring these strengths, though, is to find ways to ensure these adults are not so weighed down to the point that they never take themselves into consideration, never honor their own feelings, never ask for help.

One of the benefits of sharing experiences, in writing and in person, with others who have had similar experiences is that we can start to see when a perceived strength crosses a line into a danger zone of not attending to one's own needs.

Do children of alcoholics have scars from their childhood? The answer is "most likely," but along with the scars, there's a strong possibility they also have legacies. There's a difference between scars and legacies—scars serve no purpose other than as reminders of pain, whereas legacies are the experiential inheritances that have value . . . in other words, gifts!

. . . in and from the bad, there has been good . . .

❖ I can hear small noises at night, even when I'm sleeping
. . . if there are such things as "hearing exercises," I was
doing them all the time. Lying in bed at night, I could hear
the squeak of a cupboard door and the clink of a glass
distinctly. To this day I am sensitive to loud noises.

❖ I try to make other people happy and strive to do a good
job, to achieve and please . . . I always lived with the
hope that maybe I could make a difference in what was
happening at home. Perhaps I could talk my mother into
wanting to be sober. Perhaps if I never did anything wrong
she wouldn't drink. Perhaps I could just explain to her
what she was doing to the family. I know now that was all
folly, but it did mean that I did try to placate or mediate
situations, I did try to offer advice. I still think I can solve
other people's problems, although I'm getting better at
understanding that you can't lead anyone else's life for them.

❖ I have kept records of our children's lives through writing
early journals, filing artwork and essays, saving ticket stubs
and concert programs, and organizing photographs . . . all
so that they will be able to know about their childhoods
even if I'm not alive to tell them about them.

❖ I am responsible, have learned how to look after myself,
and can "handle" a lot, even in the absence of praise and
demonstrated love . . . from grade eight on, I became very

involved in extracurricular activities and enjoyed sports, music, and student government. Apart from enjoying these pursuits, at some unconscious level, I think I also knew that staying after school for an activity meant putting off going home. School was a place where I could receive some recognition for my efforts. Home was a situation of daily survival for everyone. There wasn't much left over for positive support or recognition.

❖ I can appreciate the psychological pain of others and understand that what you see may not be what is . . . I understand what alcohol can do to people and families and that often it's a hidden problem. I understand that we really don't know what goes on in many people's lives and so try to not make assumptions or judgments.

—⟋⟍—

P I don't know about the gifts of adversity.
I'd rather write about the gifts of genetic inheritance.
Or the gift of aging into one's parents—seeing the world through their eyes and feeling grateful to have the experience of life.

—⟋⟍—

Courage
Survival   Loyalty
Acceptance
Resilience   Adaptability
Strength
Humility
Forgiveness

I remember seeing this quote on a church bulletin board somewhere:

"An experience is what you get when you don't get what you want."

In amongst those unwanted experiences live the greatest gifts.

—◊◊◊—

Hope

- the feeling that what is wanted can be had; a longing

- a person or thing in which expectations are centered

Children of alcoholics learn early that hoping for something is often a setup for disappointment, that whatever they may have been hoping for—a day without drunken behavior; a happy family dinner; a parent attending a school play—often does not come to pass.

Some philosophic approaches to life would suggest that hoping for things is mere folly anyway and that we should all live in the moment, spending no time on reviewing the past or anticipating the future. However, the typical coping strategy of children of alcoholics is not to be so wise as choosing to "just live in the day"; rather, children of alcoholics tend to abandon expectations about what they want and reset their inner default attitude from hope to disappointment.

Years of either hoping things will be better but experiencing that they usually are not or a continuous sense of impending disappointment can lead to a personality characteristic of despair or cynicism. It takes work to learn to hope and dream again. The book *Adult Children of Alcoholics/Dysfunctional Families* has a whole chapter called "Becoming Your Own Loving Parent," which includes a number of affirmations, including, "It's OK to dream and have hope."

L Hope has cautiously returned
Hope is trying to be part of my life again
I gave up hoping for things as a teenager

Hope . . . the happy dance between what is and what can be
. . . the artful balance of having the ability to live in the moment
with an eagerness to go to the next . . . practicing not to focus on
the future but to enjoy the present and to be unafraid of what is
to come.

—⚬—

P The energy of a group often offers me hope—the little
surprise around the corner, the unexpected gift or
morsel (it sometimes feels) that, once tasted, reminds
me I have been hungry.

I used to say I didn't *do* groups—had a distrust of what might
happen to me there, or a feeling that I might be bogged down by
or imposed upon by or intruded upon by the boring, dull-witted,
diluted pap of less discerning minds. Thinking on that now, I
remember it was an Al-Anon meeting, an ACOA (Adult Children
of Alcoholics) group that changed my opinion—that in those
groups of rich, poor, well-educated, uneducated, the perfumed
and the downright smelly, morsel after morsel of hope would be
proffered by one after another of the most unexpected of people.

Hope was offered to me in that setting, and in that setting, in
an epiphany unlike anything else I've experienced, my spirituality
was unchained from my attitude about religion. I had a true "conversion experience." [See "Spirituality," pages 114–120, for my
explanation of this epiphany.]

—⚬—

Hare to hope, always . . .

Hope in yourself,

Hope in those who surround you, those who love and support you,

Hope in the gifts amidst the suffering and pain.

Trusting that you are never alone,

Hope in your Creator God,

And in so doing . . . Surrender

Humor

• the quality of being funny

• the ability to appreciate things that are funny and to laugh

---

No dysfunctional family is always without some good times, just as no healthy family is completely free of stressful times.

For children of alcoholics, it is possible to find humor in very awkward moments, and sometimes circumstances are so absurd, all one can do is laugh.

Children of alcoholics are often described as "old before their time" and, as such, have been observed to be less playful and lighthearted than their peers. When humor is found, however—whether, as mentioned below, "sick" or "silly" or "sane"— the ensuing laughter serves as an enormous and healthy safety valve, akin to steam being released from a pressure cooker.

Silly? Our parents were out. We were to make dinner for ourselves. This was fun. We made our favorite concoction with ground meat, ketchup, and other stuff. I don't really remember what the "other stuff" was and it doesn't even matter. We ate the concoction with flat egg noodles. It was yummy. But we'd made too much.

"What shall we do with the leftovers?" we mused. Without thinking very hard, we were suddenly playing with the mixture and adding outrageous things like bottle caps, corks, cigarette butts and ashes. Totally gross!

Then we made a sign and stuck it in the center with a toothpick, proudly as though it were Mount Everest and it was our nation's flag. The sign said "Custer's Last Crap!" We laughed until we almost peed our pants.

We left it on the table in the kitchen and went to bed.

Strangely enough, our parents were not amused!

Sick? My sister and I were sitting on a couch in the living room, looking out the front window, waiting for our family's doctor. A policeman was upstairs with our mother. It was only a formality because we knew she was dead. And I remember turning to my sister and saying, "Wouldn't it be funny if the Fuller Brush salesman came to the door right now and asked for our mother?" Imagining the look on his face if we told him that our mother was upstairs, but that she was dead, sent us into hysterics!

Sane? I love to lose myself in laughter. I love the physicality of it, the intensity of being in the moment, the release of tension. I need to not take life so seriously.

—ༀ—

PStop making sense.

It's all an illusion.

Feelings are like contusions.

In the end we are dust,

So what's all the fuss?

Put your body on auto.

Your mind's just a Lotto

Of risk, guess and dice roll.

Go sit on a flagpole.

Silliness, laughter, orgasm, crying,

all the same.

The convulsion of birthing.

Dark tunnel. Bright light.

Warm and watery.

Cold and hard.

I can only get to humor by being silly.

Absurd. Away from the surd.

Have a nice day.

This is not funny.

—m—

H It may be difficult to believe that there can be even a glimpse of humor found in the life of a family besieged by alcoholism. But as a mentor of mine once told me, "Life is too important to take too seriously." And in truth, I have come to believe that the ability to laugh, amidst the pain in our lives, truly saved us all from oblivion.

Certainly there have been cycles in my life when the mention of how funny my father was as he strutted around in a Santa suit one Christmas Eve filled to the gills with scotch was cause for seething anger on my part. Or the time when he was dropping hot scallops into a baggie after supper and they kept falling out the bottom as the plastic melted. He could hardly stand up, let alone take care of these poor little scallops. Not very funny then, but as I look back I find myself smiling. Not because his escapades were excusable, but because I have made peace with his desperate woundedness.

And I dare not forget the wonderful moments of sober laughter in our house. My father did have an outstanding sense of humor and, despite everything, it is through this gift of laughter that I have really begun to understand my mentor's words of wisdom.

—⁂—

Neglect

- to pay no or little attention to; to be remiss in the care or treatment of

- to omit through indifference or carelessness

- to disregard or slight

Neglect can happen as a single event or over and over again, having a significant cumulative effect. And when one has been repeatedly neglected, physically or emotionally, it is possible to grow up not knowing how to give what one never got themselves—such as love and support and a climate of safety.

It is easy to see how an alcoholic parent can be tagged with the label "neglectful," but, in fact, often the most confusing source of neglect comes from the non-alcoholic parent. It is easy to make excuses for someone who is drunk not being able to function, to nurture, or to convey love, but a child often expects that the sober parent should be able to help, protect, intervene, explain, and offer love.

The non-alcoholic parent is likely caught up in his or her own misery and desperate need to cope, as best they can. Sometimes this means just shutting down emotionally to everything and everyone, including the children in the family. For a child, this multiplies a sense of loss and neglect, and is painful and confusing.

As a child, I had a comfortable home, clothes, good food, friends, holidays by the sea. When I was twelve and had to have surgery on my hip, use crutches for a year, and then learn to walk again, there were always taxis to get me about and physiotherapy sessions. There were no visible signs of neglect. From the outside, it probably looked perfect. But on the inside there was a big, black hole of silence, of not talking, of not dealing with how anyone might be feeling.

Because I had an alcoholic mother who died when I was fifteen, I always thought my mother was the problem. By comparison, I always thought that my father was fine. Now, as an adult, I can see how wrong I was. When I think of the word "neglect," I think of my father.

My father was a man of few words unless he was the center of attention or telling a story. When my mother was still alive, we neglected to talk about her behavior, her drinking, her slurred words, her falling. We just, separately and silently, did what had to be done to cope. And when Mummy died, we neglected to talk about how we felt. It's no wonder it took me years to reach some closure around her death.

Twenty years after my mother's death, I decided I wanted to do something I'd never done . . . I wanted to visit my mother's grave. This was a big deal for me. I was nervous but also completely determined to follow through, to not chicken out. I told my father what I wanted to do during my next visit home and asked for his help in getting me the information I would need. A week before I was to arrive, I asked him again. When I got to his condo, I discovered my father had "forgotten." I asked him if he could bring home the information from his office the next day. Again, he "forgot."

I eventually called the cemetery myself and got to the office in time to be given the site number and a map. I spent half an hour looking at every gravestone in the designated vicinity but could not find where my mother was buried. A cemetery gardener helped me and concluded, "Perhaps there isn't a stone?" When I got in my car and started to drive away, I realized I was crying.

My first overwhelming feeling was one of general frustration. I had so psyched myself for this milestone and would be going home with nothing accomplished. I felt as though I'd been stood up, having had an appointment to meet someone who hadn't shown up. As my tears continued to fall, my emotional state shifted from frustration about not achieving my objective to specific frustration with my father for not helping me, for not acknowledging or honoring the importance of what I was trying to do. Before I knew it, I was in a rage. Not only was I angry about my father's repeated "forgetfulness," I was angry about what felt like a lifelong lack of emotional presence for me.

I remember going to a friend's house and storming around the kitchen and crying my eyes out. I had always been a peacemaker; I had never "done anger" before. I felt as a volcano must feel as the lava bursts forth from a bottom covered with deceptive vegetation. Like a volcano, my feelings continued to bubble up from the depths and spew forth with wild abandon.

When I returned to my father's apartment that evening, I didn't say how angry I'd been. I simply and clearly clarified how important I had felt that visiting the gravesite was going to be for me and how frustrated I felt not being able to complete my task. He said he was sorry it hadn't worked out.

A week later, my father called me long-distance to tell me he had visited the cemetery himself (his first visit ever). He discovered the reason I hadn't been able to find the grave was because he had never put a gravestone there. He had "forgotten" that too. He added, with a note of surprise in his voice, "She was only forty-eight when she died. I had forgotten that." I replied, saying that for me the number forty-eight was etched on my brain and I wondered if I would live past age forty-eight myself. He said, "That's silly." I said, "I know, but it is what I think." This was one of the most revealing conversations we'd ever had.

Does "neglect" infer an intention to choose to not do something or rather a mindless absence of intention? Did my father purposefully neglect to acknowledge that the circumstances of our family might be something I could have benefitted from talking about, or did he just presume that talking wouldn't change anything? Did he specifically choose to not reassure me that Mummy's drinking was not my fault, or was he just too wrapped up in coping himself to have anything left over to notice a child? Did he actively choose to not talk with me after Mummy died to see if I was OK, or was it just that he was caught up in his own grief? Did he make an active decision to not help me find my mother's grave, or was it just that he thought the whole idea of graves was of no significance? Thirty-five years after her death, when I asked him how the last five years of Mummy's life were for him, did he really not care to know, by asking me back, what those years were like for me, a young teenager, or did he presume everything was fine because I had never complained?

In fairness, my father was kind to me on a number of occasions. He brought me to Halifax when I started university; he visited me in the hospital when I was twenty; he took action when, as an adult, I said I would not come home anymore if my stepmother continued to be drunk by noon; and he came to Halifax for the election nights both times I ran for political office. One voice says, *These are the signs of love you are looking for,* but another voice counters with, *You needed more than signs along the way; you needed fuel.*

Strangely enough though, even with all of her drunken stupors and in spite of all my confused feelings about her, I really felt Mummy loved me. On the other hand, I do not recall my father ever saying he loved me, nor do I recall him ever saying I made him happy or proud. His friends have told me that he was proud of me, that he did care, and that he loved his visits with my family after my stepmother, his second wife, died. The adult part of me tries to embrace these third party accounts, but the child within me feels as though I've been handed a teddy bear with no stuffing. Voices in my head try to explain that he did not get up every morning willfully intending to be emotionally unavailable, or that he was just unable, or that his style was a characteristic of men of that generation, but my heart cries like a baby, desperately seeking nourishment.

Three months before my father died, I had purchased some anniversary cards for him to choose from, to send to one of his stepsons. He told me, in no uncertain terms, they were all inappropriate. Something broke inside. I told him, with my voice cracking with emotion, that I had tried, for my whole life, to make him happy and proud of me but that I didn't know what to do anymore. I told him I felt as though he always discounted or criticized any suggestions or efforts I made and so I was going to stop trying. I said I'd hit empty. He said nothing in reply.

I have a huge sense of sadness about all of this. When I think of my relationship with my father, my eyes still fill with tears and my throat goes into spasm. I hope time will bring me enough compassion to soften the edges of pain I feel.

—ɯ—

HOne of the more damaging nouns that should never be allowed to become a verb is "neglect." By definition, as a noun, it implies passivity by those who were raised by an alcoholic parent. But when "neglect" becomes a verb, it takes its rightful place among other action verbs such as to abuse, to injure, or to harm. I am not sure if there is another word in the English language that has more far-reaching effects. Alcoholics have the innate ability to turn negligence into a perverse kind of art form.

I once waited a week before someone took me to get an X-ray of my injured arm, which turned out to be broken . . . physical neglect.

I once left a note in the front hall telling my dad that I was running away—most kids do this at one time or another—but hours later when I returned, the note lay in the same place . . . unread and me unnoticed . . . emotional neglect.

God was never mentioned in our house. Church was for weddings and funerals (perhaps). But any questions I had about the source of my being were left for me to ponder alone . . . spiritual neglect.

There is nothing more frightening to a child than not being seen or heard or, even more importantly . . . not believing that they even deserve to exist on this earth.

—⟋⟍—

Resolution

- the subsiding or termination of an abnormal condition

- to deal with conclusively; to settle or solve

One of the wonderful possibilities from reflecting on one's life is that moment of coming to understand that one has a choice to hold on to pain . . . or to move on.

Moving on may take the form of asking questions that were never spoken in childhood—and answers may or may not be forthcoming. In the absence of answers, then one has to determine whether to continue to struggle with the unresolved questions or to let them go.

Moving on can manifest as forgiveness, offered directly, or simply internalized and then released.

Moving on can be seen in new understanding of the perspective of other family members and appreciating that everyone was caught up in the family pain.

The concept of "resolution" is not just tied to the options of moving on cited above. Resolution can also come as a result of being gentle with oneself and learning to appreciate the legacies from a childhood colored by alcoholism.

Often these forms of resolution are considered and reached in some form of group process, even if the group is as small as two people who can tell their stories and empathize with shared memories.

L This word has a ring of finality to it—as in "something that becomes fully resolved"—but my experience is that resolution, like so much in my life, is a continuous process, a series of doors that open into rooms with more doors leading into more rooms. I'm nowhere near running out of doors and rooms.

I may have believed I had reached resolution with my mother's death a few months after it happened, when my day-to-day life emerged with a new context and schedule that seemed fine. What I did not know, of course, is that I would grieve deeply again many times, and many years later, when I so longed to talk to a mother about marriage, about having babies, about being a parent, about what I was like when I was little, about who she really was inside her heart and soul. I miss her, even now.

Ten years ago, I thought I had achieved resolution around my frustration and anger with my father's apparent lack of emotional presence and lack of appreciation for or respect of my emotional needs. Back then, my rage exploded like volcanic lava spewing forth as a result of his completely not helping me find my mother's grave. But amidst the tumultuous experience of expressing my anger with friends came an understanding that his intention was not malicious. He did not choose to be emotionally unavailable to me; he just was himself. And I began to understand the word "acceptance." But, as I have been learning since, there are deeper feelings, pain, and frustration that still emerge.

And then there's me and my family and friends . . . here, now . . . my main practicum, the place and the people with whom I demonstrate what I've learned and what I still don't know. This seat of intimacy is, slowly but surely, providing enough love and safety for me to peel back the layers of my own being. Like an onion, some layers are gossamer thin and easy to explore and others are tough and thick and take more work to get beyond to allow me to go deeper toward the center of my being.

I am a work in progress. Therefore, the word "resolution" is not an image of being the end of a road but rather only a series of circular paths and even some sharp turns in my personal journey.

—⟊—

Hesolution speaks to me of healing into a place of forgiveness, of quiet acceptance, and of embracing all that I am because of where I have come from, not despite it. It is an ongoing process, and it was a great relief to me when I realized that I was not going to "get there." It was never going to be all finished in the classic sense of the word. My hope lies in a resolution which allows me to fully celebrate where I have been, where I am now, and where I am going!

—⟊—

Shame

- the painful feeling arising from awareness of something dishonorable or improper

- a fact or circumstance bringing disgrace or regret or humiliation

---

A sense of shame is common among children of alcoholics, as they often feel responsible, in some way, for their parent's alcoholism. They take on the weight of responsibility even though they are not the cause. Some children of alcoholics carry this sense of shame and feeling responsible forward into adulthood, by apologizing for everything, even for things that are not their fault.

Shame is a deep sense that we are flawed, that we have failed our parents, that we are guilty of everything that has gone wrong. Even when children in alcoholic families have tried so hard to be good, to be smart, the messages they received were often that they had not been good enough. Think of a child coming home, when told to, at five o'clock and being told, "Well, if you'd been here a half hour ago, you could have helped me pick your father up off the floor." Or another child who proudly presents a report card showing that he or she has come second in the class and being chastised with the question, "Why didn't you come first?"

The other face of shame is that children often feel embarrassed by their alcoholic parent and his or her behaviors. Again, while a child cannot control a parent's excessive drinking, they still bear the brunt of the situation, feel the need to apologize for the inappropriate behavior, and experience the humiliation of others' judgment or insults.

L I was twelve or thirteen. We were on a summer holiday, staying at a wonderful resort in Maine. This place was new for us. When we first arrived and drove around the grounds, I remember smiling with delight—this place would be good for me and fun for everyone in my family. It had tennis courts, boats, a bowling alley, a golf course, and two pools.

We used to rent a house in Chester, Nova Scotia, for our summer holidays but I had had hip surgery and was not allowed to bear weight on my left leg. I had to use crutches for a year. I couldn't navigate wharves or beaches, but I could get into pools.

My surgery was sudden and had taken place in May. Because we rapidly had to change our summer plans to find a vacation spot with a substantial pool, we were late booking at this resort and couldn't get one of the many family cabins on the grounds. We had to stay in something that was like a motel with twenty-four rooms. My parents were in one room, my sister and I in another room, and then strangers in the other twenty-two rooms.

The first night was OK. We were all tired and went to sleep quickly. But the second night was awful. After my sister and I went to bed, my mother got really drunk and began to yell and scream at my father and throw things. The walls were thin. I knew the people in the other twenty-two rooms could hear everything, and none of it was pleasant. Beyond my embarrassment, I was terrified that we would be asked to vacate the premises and go home.

As I crutched my way into the dining room the next morning, I felt the burning shame that comes when eyes of strangers look at you and say, "They must be the ones!" I wanted to disappear.

—w—

POf course I was ashamed of my alcoholic family for not being perfect: that mythical standard—perfection—against which (as children and adults) we measure ourselves. Being ashamed, of course, I didn't talk about my feelings about my family as I developed into adolescence. Instead I bore the feelings and kept up the appearance of being from a perfect family, or at least "doing perfectly well, thank you."

I suppose this isn't what I was thinking. I was probably thinking, *What would people think of me if they knew?* No. I think, in a way, it is more profound. I grew up with a sense of community and culture—upper-middle-class Catholic—where my sense of things was that there was absolutely no latitude for being different.

The difference of my family (alcoholic, and therefore problematic, disrupted, unhappy) was simply inconceivable. I knew no one with problems. Problems had never been presented as acceptable, normal, in any way admissible. There was no way, nowhere, and no one to absorb the difference.

And so, being ashamed became a lie, the lie of "no problem," the lie of not mattering, the lie of not feeling, not being a problem. But shame embeds itself in the psyche as a hot ember of insecurity, anger, and defensiveness that smolders until it is exposed. And once exposed to air, shame is fanned into anger or addiction until it burns away the defenses, becoming depression, that drearily common manifestation of self-hatred. At least this is how my shame is.

—⟋⟍—

H I once read that guilt is what we can speak about and shame is the darkness deep inside left unspoken. There was a lot of shame in my house as a child. What is confusing now as I look back is what shame belonged to whom? How much of the shame I carry today—some having risen to the surface, but some still lurking in hidden places inside of me— rightly belongs to my father? I think part of my "job" became to share in his shame despite the fact that now, as an adult, I can see that I was in no way responsible for his behavior. But try explaining that to a young, fearful child or a confused, insecure adolescent.

While I have faced the shame in my psyche of embarrassment, humiliation, and mistaken responsibility, I am only just beginning to confront it in the depths of my soul. As I continue on this path, one thing, if nothing else, has become crystal clear to me . . . the true healing from the woundedness wrought by shame is to be found through the forgiveness of others, oneself, and God.

—◌◌—

Siblings

- a brother or a sister or combinations

It is a source of unending fascination how different people in one family can have completely different recollections of a single event. Consequently, siblings in a family with alcoholism may not have the same interpretation of shared experiences. This also means that siblings suffer differently. As well, siblings do not necessarily support each other, sometimes thinking that one sibling is favored over others, leading to jealousies and additional pain.

In some circumstances, though, siblings do band together and look out for each other, even protecting each other. At the other end of the spectrum, siblings can just ignore everything going on around them and find their own ways of leaving, literally or figuratively, and not addressing what is happening.

Some researchers have labeled different roles siblings might take—"family hero," "lost child," "scapegoat," "mascot"—but, of course, as with all labels, they can describe but they can also limit one's understanding of one's own family. As children of alcoholics get older, siblings who haven't talked about their shared past often start to compare memories and perspectives. These conversations have the potential to lead to deeper understanding and empathy and to healing old wounds that were grounded in limited perspectives or hurt feelings.

—⁂—

L I once read a novel by Janette Turner Hospital called *The Tiger in the Tiger Pit*. As the story advanced, offered through the different memories of common events of three siblings and their father, I came to understand and appreciate that members of the same family can have divergent recollections.

I have one sister. We're a lot alike and also very different. Our memory reservoirs hold similar stories but also hold perspectives and tales in languages that one or the other of us does not know or understand.

We live on different coasts and haven't seen each other frequently in our adult years and so one can imagine the giggles of delight when we've had the experience of taking our change purses out of our bags only to discover they were exactly the same . . . same design, same make, same color! But we also have experienced the painful challenges that come from having different and unique memories that have at times played themselves out as judgments and misunderstandings.

My sister is four and a half years older than I am. She didn't have a bigger sister to look up to and I was never the oldest. I have lots of warm memories of things we did together when we were young, like making cookies together, counting out pretzels to make sure we had an even half of the package, brushing her hair, dressing our dog in clothes, playing "Alphabet" and "Moo" in the backseat of the car on long road trips, and lots of laughing.

My sister has helped me a lot in life and, as the saying goes, "she's been there for me." She arranged for a surprise party for me when I turned sixteen, she made my dresses for graduation, she took me to my driving test, she gave me words of encouragement on my wedding day, she visited when our first child was born and made me a big bag to carry all the paraphernalia that babies seem to need, she took charge when I had a miscarriage during a visit out west, she listened and knowingly recommended a regimen of vitamins when I was so stressed I was sick, and she told me I'd done a good job when we moved our father from his home of twenty-five years to a new apartment.

My sister is an amazing person who has done a lot and can do, in my view, almost anything she sets her mind to. I am awed by her knowledge, skills, and experiences, and have bragged about her accomplishments to my friends.

But against this backdrop of goodness, comfort, and admiration, there has also been jealousy, pain, and resentment. For example, I can remember vividly feeling hurt and as though I didn't matter to her when she chose to get married while I was writing a final exam at university, a week before I could get home. As I think back on this event now, remembering the angst that surrounded the event in terms of our father's reaction to the pending marriage, it may have been the first time she specifically wrapped me up into the package of pain and anger directed toward our father.

I often felt my sister resented me. Four years ago, she told me she felt I had been viewed as the "good daughter," the one who'd done the "right" things, and, consequently, that I had been favored by our parents. I had sensed this, even though it had never been explicitly stated, and told her that at one point in my life I had even consciously chosen to not tell her too much about what I was doing because I didn't want to feed any sense of division between us. On that particular visit, at a joint tarot reading, we were told that it was time to put the past behind us. We thought it was good advice, but, in hindsight, I do not think it was fully heeded.

I always wanted my sister to like me, just for being me, but it was as though this couldn't happen because she had decided, possibly unwittingly, we were in some sort of competition. Even after the tarot reading, barbs of comparison and judgment would still erupt and prick and sting. I might mention something that was happening in my life or with the children, and I would get back something that felt like criticism and negative judgment.

I felt as though she was a boxer and I was a punching bag. As was my habitual pattern, I just tried to duck. Like a turtle, I just pulled in my head. But then I came to realize that not only was I losing in this process by denying how I felt, but it was also no way to grow our relationship.

And so one day I screwed up the courage to tell my sister I didn't want to play this game anymore and I couldn't continue to try to carry our relationship alone. I didn't choose my place in the family; it just happened. I said, "I am just me. I want to be known and judged simply for who I am."

Our relationship shouldn't be about who is winning or losing. Our relationship should be about trying to understand each other's memories and perspectives enough that they become not barriers to but foundation for mutual respect and friendship. We are getting there.

—⚬—

H People have often said to me that I am so very different from my siblings that it is hard to believe we came out of the same family. But it is not really . . . because, in fact, we all came out of different families influenced by birth order, stepmothers, grandparents or the lack thereof, and varying degrees of alcohol abuse. There are similarities in our four stories, of course, but we often have been startled by different perspectives and various interpretations of memories we have shared with each other. There have, in the past, been times of defensiveness and denial. But the years have softened us all and brought us each to our own kind of reconciliation with our father and thus each other.

—◆—

Spirituality

- the quality or fact of being spiritual

- a distinctive approach to religion or prayer

Spirituality, a deep connection with a higher power, divine mystery, or god of one's choosing, is important for many as they try to make sense out of a confusing childhood.

Even if one is not connected to a formal religious foundation, considering spirituality can lead to questions about what creates a sense of well-being, feeling peaceful, and knowing that one is not alone.

For some, this comes through prayer and meditation, for some through nourishing friendships, for some through appreciating the wonder of hummingbirds, for some through raising one's voice in song or listening to special music, and for some through serving others who are in need.

L I don't really know where to go with this word. I look at it and it's almost as if it's speaking back to me, challenging me with a sarcastic edge in its voice, saying, "So? Going to write about organized religion?" My response is, "No. Can't. Won't. Doesn't work for me."

I feel a bit sad about that, really, as I observe others who seem to find so much certainty and support from the religion of their choice. *Certainty and support would be good*, I tell myself. And I am even occasionally aware of a deep stirring in me when I find myself in a church or talk with someone who seems truly connected to their religion.

I've attended lots of different churches, looking for something that feels like a fit. But, to date, my intellect keeps me from further exploring any organized religion in any serious way. I can't get past the limiting walls, the exclusionary zones for "right beliefs and practices," the sanctimonious discrimination of those who believe something else, the hypocrisy of fighting wars over religion while talking of a peace-loving and all-forgiving god.

I may not be religious, but I am interested in spirituality. My spirituality is grounded in music, nature, and, as Betty Friedan calls them, "bonds of intimacy." A Vivaldi chorus gives me goose bumps; seeing new buds on trees in the spring, wondering where grains of sand used to live, and marveling at the elegance of giraffes makes me feel deeply humble; and those moments when two people truly click fill me with warmth and make my spirit soar.

—ɷ—

P There was a guy at an Adult Children of Alcoholics Al-Anon meeting I went to whose name was "Ted." He had a round, rosy face, a rosebud mouth, and a sincere expression. What drove me crazy about him was that he frequently mentioned God, rolling his eyes to heaven as he did so. I figured, *This guy's a Bible-thumping fundamentalist and shouldn't be shoving this "God stuff" onto the group.*

One day at a meeting, Ted told a touching story from his life. After the meeting, in a gesture I considered gracious given my distaste for his God stuff, I approached him to let him know that I was moved by his story and that I learned something about myself from hearing it. He thanked me.

Then, with less-than-kind intentions, I decided to confirm my suspicion that he was a fundamentalist nut job. I thought perhaps if I actually heard directly from him that he'd bought into all that nonsense, I wouldn't feel so annoyed by all his talk of God and rolling of eyes to heaven. I thought, perhaps, I could pity him instead. (Such was my hubris at the time.)

"You must gain a lot of strength from your religion," I said as a lead-in, expecting a positive "I do" response.

"What religion?" he asked instead.

I fumbled, "Um, well, you often reference God, and I guess I just assumed that you were a fundamentalist of some sort."

He howled with laughter until tears filled his eyes. I was dumbstruck. "Oh, my, no," he managed at last. "Why would you think that?"

"Well," I said, "you do mention 'God' quite often, and when you do, you appear to have some personal connection, and I've always pictured you relating to that kindly, bearded, white man in the sky . . ."

Again, he cracked up laughing. When he could manage to speak, he said, "I probably look reverent when I say it because I am, but what I'm picturing is somewhat amorphous. How can I explain it to you?" He was looking directly into my eyes with complete sincerity. I began to get the kind of tingling feeling that happens when I've anticipated something to be one way and realize that I have misconceived and that things are not at all as I've thought.

Ted went on, "I tend to search my emotions when I say 'God' because what I'm really referring to is perhaps the power of the group process we're involved in here or the life force which emanates as people gathering for mutual benefit as we do here . . ."

I watched his smiling pink lips moving in his sweet, sincere face, but lost the rest of his words in my own interior babble as my preconceptions about what Twelve Step people—or for that matter, anyone—mean when they say "God" crumbled. I felt like the Liberty Bell must have felt when it cracked.

I left the encounter changed forever. People could actually say the word "God" and mean something abstract, such as a force or collective unconscious? That night, I pondered this for hours. The "God" I objected to was the God I had been raised with—the Catholic God who exacted perfect behavior and sent one screaming into Hell at death if there were a "mortal" sin on the soul. Could people really believe in "God" and not have that God be at all anthropomorphic, personified, *human*? I realized that *I* had been the narrow-minded one, not Ted and not necessarily others who believe in a deity. I had been the one supplying their "God" with a gender and human-like behaviors that came from my own, now-rejected, religious upbringing.

Moreover, I myself had experienced firsthand Ted's "God," the power of the group—the help available as the result of identification with the experience of others—a phenomenon that was larger than any one individual, but contingent upon the gathering together of people for mutual benefit. A phrase kept running through my head: "Wherever two or more are gathered together in my name, there is love." That is what the group felt like: love. And they invoked the word "God" for lack of a better word with which to describe that power that happens when a group focuses the power of love to help its members heal.

This was an epiphany for me, a conversion. Me, believe in God? In Ted's "God," I did.

I had to laugh. Over twenty years an atheist, to be suddenly converted through an insight into my own biases. My friends would never believe it. So, I kept it to myself.

I learned how to say the "Our Father" at Twelve Step meetings without inwardly gagging, boiling with anger over the inherent paternalism, or harking back to needless suffering and guilt I endured during my Catholic upbringing—all feelings I'd had to fight during my time at Al-Anon meetings before hearing about Ted's God. By paraphrasing to myself what I thought was the probable meaning of the words, I came up with a new understanding of the Lord's Prayer. Here is my interpretation:

Force of Universal Creation,   *Our Father, who art in Heaven*
father and mother of us all:
energy waves or particles,
source of the initial vibration, Word,
Om, invisible but real source of existence,
which some people call "God"
in order to speak about it (You):   *hallowed be Thy name.*

As I am synchronous with
universal existence, I am guided and
directed in my existence
just as the stars in their orbits are guided   *Thy kingdom come,*
by the inclusiveness   *Thy will be done*
                                                 on earth

of the ultimate origin or source.   *As it is in Heaven*

I hope for sustenance, both physical   *Give us this day*
                                                 our daily bread

and emotional, and understand

that I will be treated as I treat others,   *and forgive us our*
                                                 trespasses

since the universe reflects   *as we forgive those*

our image back to ourselves.   *who trespass*
                                                 against us.

As I remain aware of this
I ask that the richness of my world
not cause me to develop egocentricity—   *And lead us not*
                                                 into temptation

that quality that leads me to believe
that I am The Power, or in control
of existence—a misconception causing
evil in the world, avoidable   *but deliver us from*
                                                 evil.

through the awareness
that we are not It (Source)   *For Thine is the*
                                                 kingdom

but only part of the whole, which is

greater than any one or group of us.   *and the power*

I sense, but cannot understand

the enormity and beauty   *and the glory,*

of this universal integration

of energy and form encompassing me   *forever.*

and have faith that my happiness lies in

acknowledging that I/we

originate from The Source.

So be it. So it is.   *Amen*

I began to think maybe all the people who'd lived before me who had been religious might not have been as stupid as I'd here-tofore felt. I found myself able to consider that maybe some of them had even been smarter than me—miracle of miracles—and that I might have something to learn from looking at some of the religions of humankind.

I felt liberated from old beliefs and biases. I felt for the first time as though I could really "see." I was elated. Elevated. Changed. Converted. My cynicism lifted, and I was "born again" but without any limiting constrictions of religious dogma. I was free to be. The first act of that freedom was to forgive myself for the harm I'd done to myself and other people as a result of the psychologically damaging beliefs I'd picked up, and to forgive them for "harming" me through their own psychological pro-gramming. I felt free to be free.

—∞—

HThis word, although perhaps getting a bit overused, is where my heart is now. What my life is about at this point is integrating all of my experiences, not in my head or not even just in my heart, but in my soul. I have some serious work to do with God. We're talking a lot . . . at least I am and I know that He or She is listening.

Someone once came up to me after a church service where I had done something in front of the congregation. Out of the blue, as we were standing up at the altar, he said to me, "You know, Holly, it's not that I am glad you have had tough times in your life, but you wouldn't be who you are if you hadn't." I know the truth of that in my head and I even have come to believe it in my heart. But I want to understand that in my soul.

I want to explore and personalize my relationship with my creator . . . the being who has guided me to this place, through the good times and the bad, even if I have not been conscious of it. I am conscious now. My soul, which feels very old to me in many ways, is waking up and it feels safe. It feels good!

—w—

Surrender

- to yield to the possession or power of another

- give up, forgo, renounce, capitulate

A desire to surrender can result from deep fatigue, from shouldering a load of pain and assumed responsibility that is just too heavy to carry any longer. And, sometimes, it is only when we put down such a load, we can look at it with new eyes and see it for what it is, large or small, complex or simple. And it is then we can also learn to ask for help shouldering the load and its pain . . . and to graciously accept help that is offered.

Surrender also means letting go of the notion that we can reason our way through circumstances that are beyond our control. Surrender, therefore, is, in a sense, a cousin of spirituality, touching in to the notions of letting go, learning that we are not in control of things and, truly, never have been.

The Serenity Prayer from the world of Alcoholics Anonymous speaks to the concept of surrender:

"God, grant me the serenity to accept things I cannot change,

the courage to change the things I can,

and the wisdom to know the difference."

"Surrender" . . . "to someone or something; to let go, give up, relax, admit defeat, lose" . . . not my strong suit, nor how I am traditionally perceived.

I have always been a doer, an achiever, a planner and problem solver, tenacious, stubborn, responsible, not a quitter. I am only now understanding how and when some of the seeds of these qualities were planted and fertilized in the field of my childhood.

I was convinced that if I could just be good and do well, I could make everything OK at home and get the attention and love I craved. This sense may have been chosen by me, but comments like "So, why didn't you come first?" when I'd just come second fertilized the seeds of "not quite good enough."

And these messages to constantly strive for more persisted for years. For example, fifteen years later, my stepmother replied "now you'll just have to graduate with honors" when I called, excitedly, to say I'd been elected valedictorian of my university class. I remember hanging up, deflated, saying to myself, "I have to do things for myself, not for them; they'll never be satisfied." I said it but I did not really believe myself.

Years later, reading *Way of the Peaceful Warrior* by Dan Millman, I was struck by one of its key messages about living in the moment and shedding worries about the past and the future. I physically felt the wisdom. When stressed, my mantra became "the time is now, the place is here, be happy."

It seems for years, at some level, I have *known* about the positive side of the concept "surrender," but I have *lived* as though it was to be avoided at all costs.

But something is happening to me. I want to live differently. I want to let go and relax, to give up responsibilities I have assumed for the happiness of others, to learn to relax in new ways, to let go so others can grow themselves, to learn to not care about winning or losing. I am aware, now, that I have choices, almost every moment, either to lapse into old habits or display new ways of being.

I am reorienting my head and heart toward what I now humbly perceive as the peacefulness that comes with letting go and the grace that comes with surrendering. I want to get to a new place and the journey is thrilling, albeit like a roller coaster with ups and downs and moments of confusion and fear. But I am no longer just thinking about this. I am now on the road—I am a traveller.

—m—

PAt the end of our group get-together, I'm heading for the U.S. and longing to stay in Nova Scotia. The wind is gusting, waves pounding, and I am leaving my elemental world again. Nova Scotia. Nova Scotia. Each time different. This time, my friends have aged, speak poignantly about lost youth and failing faculties. Still, there's more calm, wisdom, and peace, less destructiveness and criticism. And, the land, unchanged: always green and blue and watery.

Ah, process, the process, and me still so sad for no home. Where the heart is, but where is the heart? Split down the middle between family and friends, country versus country. How long it takes to learn the lessons and then, what a short time we have to put the learning into practice!

I am feeling raw from this exercise of describing ourselves, I think. There is so much information to process, and, it is somewhat overwhelming to be in the presence of other women who pick up on and see the behaviors, defenses, anger and secrecy I carry. It is the experience of being exposed without intending to be seen. Somewhat akin is peeling one's own skin off with a butter knife.

Writing, choosing a word and writing for ten minutes? Here I am, fifty-two years old, wanting to write since age twelve, and finally, at last, able to permit myself to begin.

The holding back! Time to surrender, to surrender to this original pain of my father's problems being the door through which I must pass to be a writer.

—m—

How can one possibly hope to surrender when living in a house where it is all you can do to survive? For me, the two words—surrender/survive—became hopelessly entangled at a young age. If I surrendered to the uncertainty, the chaos, the fear, I would surely die.

Thus sprang forth a woman from a girl trying desperately to control everyone and everything in her life because the child in her still truly believed that to do any less would mean the end of her life. Alas, and thank God, this woman, who was growing ever older, finally just ran out of steam. Holding on was killing her in every sense of the word. Enter physical, emotional, and, ultimately, spiritual support.

I believe that physical death, as we pass from this world to the next, is certainly the ultimate surrender. But in the meantime, as I have progressed on the journey, I have loosened my grip!

—m—

Unpredictability

- something not to be foreseen or foretold

- erratic, fitful, variable, uncertain

Children of alcoholics never know what the day/night will bring. "Will my parent be sober/drunk, kind/mean, nurturing/neglectful, quiet/yelling?" This unpredictability undermines any sense of confidence about plans and leads to being tentative or fearful about everything.

Given the unpredictably of the lives of children of alcoholics, it is very hard for them to learn to trust their universe or make plans. As a result, many children of alcoholics are always on edge, on guard, ready for who-knows-what. Also, as has been mentioned previously, a prevailing sense of unpredictability often leads to children of alcoholics abandoning any sense of hope.

L I remember reading and underlining these words of Dag Hammarskjöld, from his book *Markings*, when I first read them at age twenty: "Never for the sake of peace and quiet deny your experience or convictions." The sentence obviously struck a chord, but I think I'm only now beginning to understand its full meaning.

I'd never know, coming home from school each day, what would be waiting on the other side of the door. There was a time when I did, when I'd yell "I'm home!" and I'd hear a cheerful "I'm here!" But those days ended in grade six. That year was the turning point and from then on, for four and a half years, every day was unpredictable.

Sometimes Mum would be drunk and passed out somewhere and sometimes she'd have it together. I never knew. There was no pattern even though I looked for one so I could know what to expect. I tried doing things I thought would help . . . being neater, helping more, getting higher grades, speaking quietly, pouring her bottles down the drain. I know now her drinking was beyond my control, but I didn't then.

The emotional fallout from this time, the effect on my personality and how I relate to people, is profound. On one level I know there's no such thing as certainty, that control is overrated and burdensome, and that it's lunacy and emotionally damaging in the long run to avoid conflict and deny one's own feelings for the sake of "peace and quiet."

But knowing and doing/being are two different things. I'm working on learning how to actively apply what I know to what I do, to how I am. And in those moments and situations when I succeed, I smile inside and privately, quietly say "Bravo!" and cheer myself on.

Thanks, Dag, for the good advice!

—⚉—

PMaybe things were predictable sometimes in my house, but I rather doubt it. Otherwise I can't figure out why I am always surprised when I call someone, for example, and they are actually home! It surprises the hell out of me. Now, I can't tell you why exactly this is so, but I suspect that it is because nothing at my home of origin was ever exactly the same, and what was unpredictable was "normalized" so that we wouldn't feel anything about it. Consequently, I don't expect things to be as they were the last time, I don't expect people to be as they were last time, I don't expect anything to be as it was, ever. This is confusing to people who interact with me over time.

This sense of unpredictability has had huge repercussions for me and is directly connected to that strand in my web labeled "abandonment," to the one called "anger" and the one called "home." Among other things it has had the effect on me of not anticipating that what I need will be met in relationships, in physical comfort, financially or any other way. If nothing is predictable, nothing can be expected.

If a baby is hungry, cries, and is not fed, it does not expect that the need for food will be met with nourishment. There is no particular relationship between hunger and being fed. When a child watches her father almost kill himself in a fall from a window, blames herself, and is not told it was not her fault, she does not trust that the world is safe or that she is a safe and trustworthy person. If an adolescent hears parents fighting and is told that nothing is wrong, the adolescent does not trust the instinctive rising of feelings when she hears angry voices.

The denial of feelings that resulted from my alcoholic family, the glossing over of tragic moments, the undiscussed uncertainty that any given day would unfold like any other given day gave rise to a deep and abiding sense of unpredictability. Anything could happen. Anything would happen. Who knew?

On the positive side, this attitude has led me to a life of adventure and change. On the negative side, I have trouble trusting that I will be safe in the world, that love others feel for me will endure, or that I can ask anything of anyone else. Who knows?

—⟋⟍—

H Is he going to explode this time or not? Will he show up for my school play or not? Will this marriage work or not? I feel as if I grew up in the midst of a perpetual earthquake somewhere between 4.2 and 8.6 on the Richter scale.

As I look back on the inconsistency of my childhood born out of alcohol abuse (among other things), it is surely no wonder that I have had difficulty trusting. There was no emotional consistency while I was growing up, and that has been the source of profound grief for me over the years . . . particularly as I have struggled to provide stability for my own kids.

For years I had such a hard time dealing with change. I see now that I wanted and needed things to stay the same for a while and if there was ever a threat of change, I panicked. As I have grown older, however, I have begun to see my ability to adapt to uncertainty in a new and much more positive light.

Life is unpredictable. I accept that now and I honor the mysteries of what may or may not happen next. I can survive change!

—⟋⟍—

Now I have no choice but to see with your eyes.
So I am not alone, so you are not alone.

—Yannis Ritsos

Chapter 5

Your Turn

To be a person is to have a story to tell.
—Isak Dinesen

After the three of us had written our original writings, the snap-shots from our childhoods with our alcoholic parents, we con-structed a letter to invite other women we knew to participate with us in writing and sharing. Inspired by our original letter, we have crafted a new version just for you, hoping you accept our invitation to begin your own writing and your own transforming process of discovery and healing.

We hope you will say yes—yes to being willing to try writing, yes to possibly starting today. Today, you ask? Yes, today, now. You can begin to write today . . . it's not too late.

Dear Readers—
This is our "official" letter to invite you to try writing some reflections about being the child of an alcoholic [or about anything that might sit heavily on your soul] . . . .

While many discussions with good friends are intensely personal, they rarely involve the actual telling of incidents, the actual description of events or pictures that we all carry vividly in our memories.

Try writing about a memory (or several central memories) of your childhood experiences . . . memories of incidents that forever haunt you . . . and then share them with others.

If you choose to share your writing, you will also have the privilege to see others' "personal pictures." You will learn a lot about yourself and about others. And you will possibly find the process of putting your memories down on paper to be difficult but also helpful, cathartic. Fear not! Research is saying that writing about trauma is good for your health.

What you write doesn't have to be very long . . . it just needs to communicate images you remember when you close your eyes or stare off into space and think about what you went through as a child (or still go through as a child) of an alcoholic parent [or as a result of your own unique challenging circumstances in childhood]. Change names and places and write under a pseudonym if you are concerned about confidentiality.

You don't even need to worry about writing with perfect grammar and spelling. What matters is that you find your voice and capture images and emotions, your own "relivings." The computer can check for spelling!

If you are now thinking, "Tempting idea, but I think it would be too painful for me," let us counter with, "Pain can be productive if you work with it . . . this might help." If you are saying, "Tempting idea, but I don't have the time," let us counter with, "There's always time for things if you feel they are important." If an inner judge is suggesting, "Sounds like a tempting idea, but I can't write," let us counter with, "Don't let concern about writing ability keep you from doing something you want to do." And, last but not least, if you are feeling drawn to this but don't know where to begin, we have listed a variety of writing prompts or exercises to get your expressive juices flowing.

Please say yes.

Your Story Matters

We know stories will only be written/told when someone is ready. Maybe you don't feel ready, but we suggest trying a bit of writing anyway. No one is asking you to write something that would win a Pulitzer Prize, and you can always tear up what you write. You really have nothing to lose and everything to gain. Writing has an ability to open internal doors and retrieve seemingly forgotten memories. In other words, writing may show you are "readier" than you think! You will never know unless you try . . .

You may find it helpful to establish some rituals around writing . . . Somerset Maugham always wore a special hat when he wrote. You might want to establish a special place to write and a predictable time of day or night. You might want background music or complete silence. You might want to read a passage from a book of meditations or you might want to empty your mind and just jump right in. And how about having a hot cup of coffee or tea, a special pen, a favorite notebook, a comfortable chair, perhaps a candle to create a contemplative atmosphere, a timer to tell you when ten minutes have passed. When you have finished writing, you might want to identify a safe place to put your words until you are ready to share with others.

In case you don't know where or how to begin, here are twenty-five writing prompts or exercises you can use to begin. We have culled them from our own experiences and from writers we admire.

We could have come up with even more, but we think that once you begin, you will be able to come up with your own catalysts.

Quite possibly, the simplest way to begin would be to use some or all of the words in chapter 4 to evoke and capture your own memories or emotions. As a variation on this theme, you may want to make your own list of loaded words and jump right in.

These exercises are in no particular order—you can start at the beginning or read down to find something that appeals to you . . . or you can just close your eyes and put your finger on the page, randomly, trusting that that's the exercise for you at this moment.

Just start. Try writing for ten minutes at first, but feel free to write longer if the words are flowing. Remember—no rules . . . just begin.

Writing Prompts

1. If you were writing a book about your childhood, give your book a title . . . and then try writing the opening paragraph.

2. Write letters to your family members, dead or alive, and tell them who you are at this point in your life. (And remember, there is no expectation you have to send these letters.)

3. Consider that you have the opportunity to interview the people in #2. What questions would you want to ask? As you imagine what they might say, remember that an interviewer can keep asking "Why?" to enable you to get to deeper answers.

4. If you were being interviewed, what would you want to be asked? What would you *not* want to be asked . . . and why?

5. Describe where you lived as a child—and maybe try this in a bulleted list: your bedroom, your house/apartment, your neighborhood. What do you see? Can you smell anything? Are there sounds that you recall? Who was there?

6. What five words do you hope or wish people would use to describe you. Why have you picked these words?

7. Get a dictionary and just open to a page at random and put your finger down on a word . . . and then write for ten to twenty minutes. Here's an example of what happened when someone touched the word "carry":

   I have carried children before they were born and carried them
      again

   as babies, crooning them to sleep,

   as toddlers, whispering away the pain of scraped knees,

   as teenagers, giggling hysterically, trying to piggyback them
      across the room.

   I have carried small puppies new to our family,

   and then carried them again to their graves.

   I have carried cut-up food to my mother,

   hoping food could nourish her intoxicated soul.

   I have carried disappointment and resentments for years

   unaware of the magnitude of the burden.

8. As you think of various dramatic or humorous moments from your life, to whom would you give the Academy Award for Best Supporting Actor/Actress . . . and why?

9. Complete this sentence: "The first time I _____"
   (. . . and you can do this exercise over and over).

10. If you were going to be on a magazine cover, which magazine would you pick and what would the caption be? Can you write the whole article?

11. Remember something that happened during your childhood that troubled you . . . and try writing about that experience from another family member's point of view.

12. Make a list of little-known facts about you. Which of these do you love?

13. What were the gifts of your childhood?

14. Make a list of moods such as mad, glad, sad, bored, tired, anxious, etc. Take one of these moods and write about a time when you felt this way.

15. Find a picture from your childhood and write about what you see, what you remember (. . . and you can do this exercise over and over).

16. Make a "gratitude" list. From this list, is there anyone you want to write to?

17. What do you long for? What's keeping you from attaining this?

18. Think about a turning point in your life and describe it in one sentence. Stay with this reflection and go deeper . . . Who was there? Was anything said? Why did this happen? Was it by chance or by intention? What else can you say about this? How were you feeling before this turning point . . . and after? How do you feel now? Have you left anything out? Is there anything else about this turning point you can add? Are there

any connections about this turning point to other aspects of your life? (And you can keep asking yourself questions . . . it's often surprising what lies deeper in our memories as we peel back the layers.)

19. Try interviewing your body. For example, "Eyes . . . what have you seen that frightened or delighted you?"; "Ears— were things ever too loud for you?"; "Feet—were you ever too cold?"; "Heart—did you ever beat very, very fast?" . . .

20. Write a haiku—a Japanese form of poetry made up of three lines, the first and third with five syllables and the middle line with seven syllables. Here's an example:

    The cupboard opens

    Hiding forbidden bottles

    Hopes are crushed again.

21. If you only had ten minutes to write your life story, what would you include? Try it.

22. Complete this sentence: "I once thought _____ but now I know _____" (. . . and you can do this exercise over and over).

23. Imagine a movie is being made of your life. What music would you want in the soundtrack and why?

24. Go to the library, to the memoir section, and examine what people have written for their opening lines. What would you write as the opening line of your memoir?

25. Did your family have its own rituals—fish on Fridays, special cakes for birthdays, lists of chores? Pick one of these rituals and examine where it came from and how it felt.

If writing feels like a struggle and nothing is coming, change your scene—go for a walk, take a bus ride, look for things that are light or dark, observe people. This is sometimes called a practice of "losing your mind and coming to your senses" and is often effective in eliminating writing stagnation. Another option if you are feeling stuck is to try drawing a picture instead of writing. Last but not least, you can always use the statement "this is why I am feeling stuck" as your writing prompt!

Sharing

When you've done some writing, you may be ready to think about sharing your reflections with another person or with a group.

Over the years, two of the three of us found solace in joining Al-Anon where, by gathering anonymously in groups around a suggested set of principles, people can safely speak and share their stories. However, as explained in the first chapter, sharing written work is another matter and is not the same as simply talking. Writing is more profound and has more beneficial effects on your health.

We hope you will find at least one other person you trust to share your writing and to speak your words out loud. We encourage you to listen with your heart to what is offered in return. Even if you only find one other person, the beneficial effects can be profound and you will know you are not alone.

We have already suggested identifying a trusted friend, a wise colleague, people with whom you share experiences and values. If no one immediately comes to mind, you can watch for community talks or book groups that might relate to challenging childhood experiences—showing up and being in the audience might help you identify others who might be interested in sharing experiences. Try to find writing groups, perhaps through writing organizations in your community, or consider starting your own. You might even learn about and feel brave enough to attend a weekend gathering dedicated to exploring past experiences.

We were blessed with being a small group and engaged in a process that covered writing and sharing over a considerable period of time. However, one of the people who only attended our first gathering felt that even that brief weekend had been profoundly valuable. She wrote:

On Sunday morning, before we all went our separate ways, I looked around the room and saw myself—myself in the past and in the future. I saw myself struggling with wanting recognition from my alcoholic parent . . . I saw myself crying because I felt I had failed and hadn't been able to save him from himself and make everything better . . . I saw myself calm in knowing there was nothing I could have done to change the way things were . . . I saw myself older, wise and still beautiful . . . I saw myself laughing . . . I saw forgiveness of others for their being human.

I understood there was a reason we were all here together. It was like bringing together the various pieces of a whole person, the whole person I someday wanted to be, that I was becoming. And then I knew, I really knew, I was going to be all right!

When I came home, I had changed. It was subtle but I could feel it. I had discovered a certain part of me that was stronger than it had ever been and these women helped make that possible.

Worth a Try

Writing is cheap, available (even in the middle of the night), portable, doesn't need to take much time, can be private or shared, and has the power to heal trauma and improve your health! Even if you share your writing with only one other person, the beneficial effects can be profound and you will know you are not alone.

Even though our journey together, with all of its writing and sharing, spanned three decades, the benefits started right away and were sustained. We are not necessarily suggesting you begin a thirty-year process . . . but we are inviting you to at least write for ten minutes and then share what you've written with someone else. And then we hope you will try it again . . .

—∞—

It is our inward journey that leads us through time—forward or back, seldom in a straight line, most often spiraling . . . As we discover, we remember; remembering, we discover.

—Eudora Welty

Chapter 6

Living Our Legacies:
Who We've Become

I am an adult child [of an alcoholic] and I will be
one until the day I die, but I will not die one more
day because I am an adult child [of an alcoholic].

—Robert J. Ackerman

When we began, we were married or had been married, and were mothers. We all worked in one way or another—conventionally, through volunteering, or freelance work. Two of us had moved several times and one of us had lived in the same place for over twenty years.

When we started to work together, we had all outlived our alcoholic parent and had come to have one or more stepparents and stepsiblings. Two of us still had one parent alive. And now, all of our children have left home and some have had children of their own. All of our parents have died. As we were transforming our memories, the context of our lives was also transforming.

Through our process, we developed a deep appreciation of the poignancy of our childhoods and for the lives we have now. We wrote and shared in a process of emergence . . . details of emotional and behavioral legacies of our past slowly revealed themselves, like peeling back the layers of an onion. Over the years, we have tried to take it all in, pay attention, and learn as we've grown older.

Did we grow? Did we learn anything? Did we transform our memories? Did we heal? We believe the answer is yes . . . but we offer these reflections to you so you can make your own assessment.

L My mother died when I was fifteen. I've had a lot of time to think about things.

I don't think I properly grieved my mother's death for years, probably not until I was well into my twenties and then again when I became a mother myself. There were times that I really wanted a mother, someone who would give me advice and share memories and understand some of my experiences. More recently, though, I have come to realize that while I thought I had lost a mother because she had died, in reality I had lost a mother before then because she was an alcoholic. In other words, even if she had not died, my fantasies of what I would have had in a mother may never have been realized, especially if she had continued to drink.

There's no question in my mind that alcoholism is a family tragedy. The tragedy was augmented in our house because my father, sister, and I never talked about what we were witnessing, feeling, and trying to cope with. We didn't talk at the time and we didn't talk after my mother died. I'm sure we all felt terribly alone. It's too bad we couldn't figure out how to support each other.

Over time, I have become more aware of how my mother's drinking affected everyone else in our family. For years I'd been so wrapped up in what it all meant to me that I didn't really appreciate how my family members' view of things may have been different, but not necessarily any less painful . . . maybe even more so.

For a while I was hugely angry with my father for never being emotionally present for me, either as a child or as an adult. Now, I accept that he was simply who he was and that he had his own crosses to bear. I had no idea what it was like for him to have his wife become an alcoholic who died young and then be solely responsible for his two daughters.

His way of surviving or coping may have been effective for him; it just wasn't much help for me. But at least he never crumbled . . . at least I always felt that someone was able to carry on in spite of all else. While his parenting style was not emotionally nourishing, he was who he was—I accept that now.

Through the various writing exercises we did for this project, through sharing how we were functioning as adults, I became aware of some of my habitual behaviors, my default reactions that were well practiced in my childhood and carried through to adulthood. In other words, I have come to have a better view and understanding of the legacies of my childhood. For example, I acknowledge that I still dislike conflict and try hard to make everyone happy when there is discord; but I am learning to not run away from tension, to claim my feelings, and to constructively confront challenging situations.

I also know that I sit on the overachiever end of the spectrum, likely stemming from taking on adult responsibilities while still a child and doing what I could to solve the "problem" of my mother. Being an overachiever is not all bad, and I have been able to accomplish much, learn a great deal, and, hopefully, contribute to my family and my community.

I remember, as a child, trying so hard to be nicer, smarter, faster, quieter—whatever I could do to make things better. And sometimes I can see I am still that child, trying so hard to do so much. I am deeply aware of the need to make sure there is balance in my life between "being busy" and "simply being." I am striving to be responsible for less, focus on things over which I have some control, and let the others go. Old habits die hard, though, and achieving a balanced life and a life of appropriate responsibility is a constant struggle.

I have always been drawn to support others who are experiencing literal or figurative pain and problems in life. I suspect this inclination is also rooted in my childhood, wanting so badly for everyone to be happy and also having some deep appreciation of the need for support in the face of traumatic events.

However, sometimes my idea of support has looked more like trying to solve someone's problems. I am learning that supporting is good, but solving is not my role; it simply comes from old behaviors of wanting problems to go away. I've come to realize that it's often appropriate, and maybe even important, for people to experience pain and sadness and a sense of loss. In many cases, support is often best offered through quiet listening, through bearing witness.

Even with my desire to offer support, which I consider to be a positive trait, I can find myself doing so much for others that I may shortchange myself and not have enough time for what I and those closest to me might need. It would be wise to remember the first rule of first aid, which is to not put oneself at risk. I need to remind myself that one of my favorite quotes is "we nourish from overflow, not emptiness" and pay attention to my "almost empty" mark.

People know me as someone who cries easily and for years I have been trying to figure out why this is the case. I have observed that I typically cry in response to stories of exquisite kindness and tender love, or to recalling profound moments of loving and being loved, or to witnessing expressions of a deep sadness from the lack of love or love lost. I recently had a possible epiphany which is this: it occurs to me that the reason I am so touched by these "love moments" is that I had a big hole to fill up, the hole created in childhood from not believing I was enough or worthy of love. Recognizing this is helping me to receive love graciously, with both gratitude and delight, and to offer it purely, not because I want to change someone.

At this stage in my life, I feel deeply humbled. I am humbled because I have come to understand and appreciate how many people have experienced alcoholism in their families and/or other aspects of dysfunctional family dynamics. I am humbled by a certain degree of "ordinariness" of my childhood.

I am also humbled because I realize that I have been blessed with relatively good health, opportunities for education and meaningful work, wonderful friends, a curious mind, a forty-four-year loving marriage and two kind, loving, interesting and funny children, and a family of origin that meant well and tried to do its best. While many aspects of my childhood did not live up to a Hallmark card of "ideal family," at least I had enough going for me that I survived the uncertainty, the unpredictability, the shame, the moments of fear, and the early death of my loving and alcoholic mother.

—〰—

P Before we began the process of writing about being children of alcoholics, I hadn't truly considered, in any depth, the impact my upbringing had had on me. I was stoic, and thought that was simply my personality. I felt that I was "up to the task," whatever it was, and that I really didn't need help from any quarter. A rigid independence and a tamping down of feelings served me well because I was a single, working mother and needed to simply keep my head down and stay on task with whatever was at hand. Or, so I thought.

To that date, motherhood had been my proudest membership and greatest accomplishment and remains so to this day. But as my son left home and moved into the world on his own, I found I had to confront a really big question: Who am I now that I am not primarily my child's mother? My attempts to address that question included doubling up on an already full workload as I completed a second graduate degree while, at the same time, continuing to work long hours as a largely self-employed independent contractor. I simply continued being Superwoman, which was how I'd always thought I should be.

Meanwhile, the writing I'd done with our loaded words had got under my skin to the extent that I continued to explore the impacts of my childhood on me as an adult. I began to offer myself increased understanding and compassion. Suddenly I was "allowed" to be vulnerable. I guess that now that I no longer had a child to parent, I was re-parenting myself, to use the parlance of psychotherapy.

The most radical result of my increased self-understanding was the end of many years of "stiff upper lip" and "bootstrap" coping as I learned how to allow my feelings and my vulnerability to emerge. Instead of the "can do" façade I'd always worn, I found myself allowing that I couldn't do everything, manage everything, be everything. This humbling was hard-won, and often hard to take at first. Hard for me to take, that is, having long suppressed emotions—particularly the negative ones such as fear and anger, and the uncomfortable ones like confusion and bewilderment.

I continued seeking and exploring meaning, transcendence, knowledge, and now, also, feeling. Once I'd added "feeling" into my repertoire (no longer the Stoic), I became better equipped to reveal myself, to take the risks of sharing myself with others. The Aquinas quote "first to be, then to give" comes to mind. I began to change; to really appear before others, to show up—visible, vulnerable, all too human.

In recent years I've come to reconcile the sense of frustration and lack of fulfillment I felt as a child with what I know to be true: that my mother was a loving, supportive presence as much as she could have been with four children whose ages spanned eighteen years and a rambunctious alcoholic for a husband. Certainly my father was emotionally neglectful, involved as he was with alcohol, and he did cause pain and embarrassment. But he was not a bad man; he was a trapped man, hopelessly addicted. And probably my mother (bless her heart—and please forgive me here, Mom), involved as she was with my father's alcoholic behaviors, leaned on me as an ally a bit overmuch, not realizing that my stalwart alliance as her confidant had, in a sense, catapulted me into adulthood much too early. As my father's alcoholism blossomed, feeling much older than the preteen, than the early teen that I was, I developed a sense that I had to partner with my mother, to help her with her concerns about my father. I became "parentified."

For the balance of my life since then, I've been revisiting the transformative central event of my life: the night, at age eleven, my father fell from a window because I could no longer hold him inside. As years have passed, new understanding has evolved and continues to evolve. After all this time I know this to be true: my father's alcoholism was not a result of the terrible accident he suffered that I long thought was my fault. Rather, he had most likely developed an alcohol problem early in life, as a young man, and it had overtaken him at some point in his early middle age. My mother, herself, was no stranger to alcoholic family systems; her own father's alcoholism had caused the breakup of her own family of origin when she, herself, was a youngster.

I continue to piece together remembered swatches of the fabric of my childhood with new revelations to construct the patchwork I understand to be me. Now, from long years of habit, I do it by writing my thoughts down in story form. Decanting thoughts into sentences on a page is very different from keeping the words in thought form. I read the stories I write and discover more and more about who and what I am. That said, I think the most helpful thing about the *loaded words* project, from first gathering to write together up to the present, has been identifying with others who have come from similar emotional circumstances and learning that whatever I have suffered, I am not alone.

Who am I now? I'm just a person: sometimes bewildered, sometimes clear, always learning. I am a mother, of course, and now a grandmother. I've acquired a life partner, which is a direct result of learning and acknowledging more about myself, my needs, and my feelings. I've had rewarding careers—all of which hold the common element of service through storytelling.

Liz, Holly, and I have decided to put some of our stories in this book for you to read in hopes that by reading how we've told them and the process we went through to be able to tell them, you might be encouraged to begin to tell your own story your own way.

All these years after first working with the idea of loaded words, I understand much more about my family of origin, about life, and about myself. I'm a better person for it, happier and healthier, with an abundant share of emotional and spiritual wealth.

—◦◦◦—

HI came to our first gathering with a quiet enthusiasm for our project but, in retrospect, not much energy. I was still reeling from a number of deaths that had impacted my life over the previous months.

In particular, when we first got together, it was only ten short days after accompanying a dear friend on her last days on earth. She had died from the ravages of cystic fibrosis at the tender age of thirty-three. Our paths had crossed in my work as a palliative care chaplain. I started to recognize some profound connections between my friend's death, the gathering itself (which raised lots of old issues), my health which deteriorated after I returned home, and leaving my job.

One of the most deeply entrenched legacies left to me as an adult child of an alcoholic has been that of *conditional* love, never being truly able to believe that I am lovable just because of who I am, as opposed to because of what I do. Consequently, I spent years as a child, followed by years as an adult, literally killing myself while trying to get people's love and approval. I have taken care of everyone and everything, in my orbit and beyond, to ensure my survival. And the paradox has been that even though I tried so hard to get people to love me, I couldn't let love in. I was too scared. What a tremendous case of misspent energy.

But then my friend died, I came to the gathering, I got sick, I quit my job, and I began to learn. I began to see more clearly that my soul was exhausted. I absolutely had to let go of some of my fear and my mistaken beliefs. My friend, unknowingly, gave me permission to begin.

This woman loved me so much . . . no strings . . .

And I loved this woman . . . with an open heart . . .

Knowing our time together would be short;

Not doing anything to earn her love;

I just loved her and she loved me . . .

Then she died . . . and I survived.

By the time I arrived at our second gathering, my body and soul were beginning to heal. I arrived with enthusiasm that was a trifle louder than before and an energy level that was on the upswing. I continued to remind myself that it was OK to be gentle with myself.

And then I went on a wonderful eight-day retreat with God. Just the two of us. No big agenda, no issues or goals. Just being together in the moment, experiencing life and unconditional love—something it had taken me forty-three years to really start to taste. And let me tell you . . . it was sweet! Clearly, I needed to retreat to engage!

When we began this project, I was forty-three, but I felt I had a soul older still. My "young girl" was starting to be no longer frightened of being truly seen. As a wife, I was slowly opening myself to being loved just for who I was, not for what I did. As a parent, I still struggled with perfection and I still quietly mourned the loss of my own childhood, all the while being continually overwhelmed with the incomparable gift of my three children. I was also aware of being a child of God—stumbling along, searching, seeking, laughing, crying, resisting, but moving ever closer to letting go, to surrendering.

And now, I have come ever closer to understanding the truth in Mark Nepo's words from *The Book of Awakening* that "our essential nature is not changed, only enhanced." Have I grown? Most certainly. Does the transformation continue? Always. Is my essential nature enhanced? I hope so.

Still, I am the same woman in many ways, that Child of God who is stumbling toward enlightenment; searching and seeking, laughing and crying, resisting and letting go, always hopeful that a more complete surrender to the Divine Mystery is right around the corner.

Fear is quieter in my life, and expectations of others and of myself continue to melt away. Every day I pray for the ability to humbly accept whatever presents itself.

And what about that prickly word that trips us up; what about love? While my heart has opened more fully to receiving and giving love, and I believe more deeply that I am, in fact, worthy of love, my old patterns of emotional reactions and behavior can be triggered in a heartbeat. I can find myself wallowing in old mistaken beliefs that I am not good enough, and that I need to do something to earn love.

At least now I recognize the roots of my insecurity. With new awareness, I can turn the flow of unhealthy emotions around and save the integrity of my day. When I am experiencing old fears or find myself feeling like a victim, I have tools to turn things around. This path of deep healing has opened space in my soul to let unconditional love in and remind myself that I am lovable.

Perhaps the greatest gift of this journey toward wholeness has been that I have embraced my woundedness. Doing this has been a tremendous gift and has empowered me to break the dysfunctional cycle of my childhood that I had carried into my adult life. I have written a new script and, though not without its flaws, this revised life story is filled with honesty, and hope, and I am surrounded by loving support. I know I am not alone.

My life journey has taken me all over the emotional map since we first came together over thirty years ago. This process, however, was one of my earliest experiences of sharing my pain with the intention of opening the door to deeper healing.

It takes courage to dive into those dark corners of our lives; places that we keep hidden from ourselves and others. The pain I had carried for so long had become familiar. It was scary to even imagine the repercussions of taking the cork out of the bottle that had kept those feelings safe for so long. Touching those tender places can lead to unending questions: Who am I without my pain? Will I completely fall apart if I confront my issues? Can I bear to relive the suffering?

But holding onto the pain was slowly sucking the life out of my soul. It became clear that healing would only happen if I could find the strength to get honest with myself. Working with our loaded words and with Liz and Polly put the smallest of cracks in my heart and the light began to get in.

There were many gifts that emerged out of this experience over the years, and that small crack got bigger. Most important was the newfound understanding of the value of sharing my pain and being a witness to the pain of others. There had been a lot of secrecy in my home, and being involved with this project led me to feel safe enough to tell pieces of my story without judgment and encouraged me to continue on the path to wholeness.

The group process also brought awareness to the reality that I was not responsible for the stories of others. It was not my job to fix or help or to try to take away their pain. Instead, I began to learn how to simply listen, and this was cause for celebration!

As a hard-core caretaker, detaching from the pain of others continues to be a struggle for me, but staying on this path has led me to a clearer awareness of my old behaviors. I have the ability to change direction when I jump on the problem-solving train, and seek a healthier balance.

As the journey of what has become *Transforming Memories* unfolded, our circle became smaller—from seven to three—and therein lay another gift for me. I began to learn how to honor the paths of others. Historically, I had unrealistic expectations of people, and felt compelled to move them along the path *I* thought was best for them—a particularly arrogant character defect! There is nothing more helpful than the dynamics of a group to curb that compulsion.

At the end of the day, I am most grateful for this experience. *Transforming Memories* uncovered a path for me that might never have come to light. It has opened me to countless healing scenarios over the years.

And while it may have taken thirty years for our original intention to become a reality, my last lesson is to remember that all will unfold in the fullness of time. Trying to push the river never works. Trusting the timing of Divine Mystery always does!

—⁓—

Abraham Lincoln, in his 1861 inaugural address, urged the United States to come together, penning the phrase "the better angels of our nature." We believe, even if dark memories and old wounds appear to stand in the way, we can all find these better angels of our own nature. We believe the fruits of our writing exercises and our process of sharing how we have brought legacies from our childhoods into adulthood has helped us find our better angels. Each of us has participated in the making of this book to contribute, in some way, to encouraging you to find your better angels and to the general life force that unites all positive human endeavors.

—∿∿—

The adventure of life is to learn.
The goal of life is to grow.
The nature of life is to change
The challenge of life is to overcome.
The essence of life is to care.
The secret of life is to dare.
The beauty of life is to give.
The joy of life is to love.

—William Arthur Ward

Chapter 7

Reflecting . . .

To see takes time.

—Georgia O'Keeffe

It is difficult to imagine that there's anything left to say . . . and yet our learning, stemming from living in alcoholic households as children, continues every day. Hopefully, it is obvious that we believe we benefitted enormously from all the writing and sharing we did. There's no going back!

On further reflection and in no particular order, here are some additional observations we share with you:

❖ One should never confuse "discovery" with "recovery"; *admitting* what happened is not the same as *processing* what happened. As children we coped with our situation; at midlife we were accommodating our pasts and beginning to admit what had happened but were only starting to discover that we were wounded. Now, from the perspectives of our later years, we are learning what recovery feels like, and how to discard old habits and judgments and be patient with ourselves. The journey from discovery to recovery can be done alone but is faster, more interesting, and more effective to take with others. An African proverb captures this: "If you want to go fast, go alone, but if you want to go far, go together."

❖ What we learned when we did our original writings was revealing, both to ourselves and each other. Reflecting back now, years later, even more has been revealed. Our process enabled us to have a deeper appreciation of how our childhood experiences continue to shape what we see, what we feel, what we understand . . . layers and layers . . . still peeling back to reveal more.

❖ We shed the secrecy and shame of our childhoods and learned that we were not alone. We were comforted by this knowledge and the sharing that ensued, but we know there are so many who still struggle in silence.

❖ We are still learning to let go, to try to control less (ideally nothing), to let love in, to believe we are worthy. We all feel we are making progress.

❖ Our process was, essentially, leaderless. Often groups have a designated leader, or a leader emerges. Given that all of us admit our natural tendency toward needing to control things, it is amazing that we all seemed to let go of that need and trust the process to naturally unfold.

❖ Our process wasn't just about recalling our memories; it was about coming to understand the behaviors, feelings, and habits that resulted from them. These understandings created the foundation to enable us to build new responses and patterns.

❖ Self-analysis is one thing . . . but one's analysis is richer and deeper when shared with others who help you see your emotional patterns and behavior habits that you can't see on your own.

❖ It was often emotionally difficult to revisit our memories through writing, but "difficult" doesn't mean one should "avoid." We may have occasionally struggled to open up and go deep, but in the end it was so worthwhile—even a relief!

❖ In the beginning, we thought we were just getting people together to create a book . . . we didn't understand the power and importance of the actual process we were in, which included not only writing, but also sharing and listening and being honest and vulnerable. It has been such a privilege to walk with others on this shared path.

—✺—

Our hope is that you will write and will also find a way to share your writing. And even if you've never had a problem in your life, still write, still share . . . Who knows what you will discover? And if your stories are only of lovely moments and loving memories, we can all be enriched by your pictures of positive possibility.

The following poem is our final gift to you—we believe it captures deep truths.

ALLOW
There is no controlling life.
Try corralling a lightning bolt,
containing a tornado.
Dam a stream
and it will create a new channel.
Resist, and the tide will sweep you off your feet.
Allow, and grace will carry you to higher ground.
The only safety
lies in letting it all in—
the wild and the weak;
fear, fantasies, failures and success.
When loss rips off the doors of the heart,
or sadness veils your vision with despair,
practice becomes simply bearing the truth.
In the choice to let go of your known way of being,
the whole world is revealed
to your new eyes.

—Danna Faulds

———

*If I am not for myself, who will be for me? If I am not
for others, who am I for? And if not now, when?*

The Talmud

Appendix A

The Benefits of Spontaneous/ Expressive Writing

Selected Research Studies

Owning our stories means reckoning with our feelings and rumblings with our dark emotions—our fear, anger, aggression, shame, and blame. This isn't easy, but the alternative— denying our stories and disengaging from emotion— means choosing to live our entire lives in the dark.

—Brené Brown

In addition to studies mentioned in chapter 1, here are some others we have found worthy of investigation, starting with the most recent. It is now possible to find hundreds of studies through searching the Internet or referencing the bibliographies in some of the books we cite in appendix B.

❖ In a study done with students trying to adjust to college at Stanford, participants in the experimental group were asked to create an essay or video. This group received better grades in the ensuing months. (This study was recently referred to in a *New York Times* blog column titled "Writing Your Way to Happiness" by Tara Parker-Pope on January 19, 2015.)

❖ In a study of nearly 1,300 returning veterans, those who completed online expressive writing sessions showed more improvement than peers who had not written at all or had only done factual writing. Beneficial effects among those who completed expressive writing sessions included reductions in physical complaints, anger, and stress. See N. Sayer, S. Noorbaloochi, P. A. Frazier, J. W. Pennebaker, K. J. Orazem, P. P. Schnurr, M. Murdoch, K. F. Carlson, A. Gravely, and B. T. Litz, "Randomized Controlled Trial of On-Line Expressive Writing to Address Readjustment Difficulties among US Afghanistan and Iraq War Veterans." *Journal of Traumatic Stress* 28, no. 5 (2015): 381–390.

❖ In a study of 277 patients with renal cell cancer, participants were randomly assigned to two groups and asked to write on four separate occasions. The first group was asked to write about their deepest thoughts and feelings about their cancer (expressive writing) and the other group was asked to write about neutral topics (neutral writing). Using various measures, the study concluded that expressive writing may reduce cancer-related symptoms and improve physical functioning in renal cell cancer patients. See K. Milbury, A. Spelman, C. Wood, S. F. Matin, N. Tannir, E. Jonasch, L. Pisters, Q. Wei, and L. Cohen, "Randomized Controlled Trial of Expressive Writing for Patients with Renal Cell Carcinoma." *Journal of Clinical Oncology* 32, no. 7 (2014): 663–670.

❖ In Auckland, New Zealand, forty-nine seniors, ranging in age from sixty-four to ninety-seven, agreed to have a small skin biopsy done. Half of them wrote for twenty minutes a day about a trauma while the others did no writing at all. By the end of sixteen days, among the writers, 76 percent of the wounds were completely healed while among the nonwriters, only 42 percent of the wounds had healed. See H. E. Koschwanez, N. Kerse, M. Darragh, P. Jarrett, R. J. Booth, and E. Broadbent, "Expressive Writing and Wound Healing in Older Adults: A Randomized Controlled Trial." *Psychosomatic Medicine* 75, no. 6 (2013): 581–590.

❖ A study from the University of Chicago found that when students were given ten minutes to write about their feelings about a pending test, their marks improved by 5 percent while in the group that sat quietly, their scores worsened by 12 percent. See G. Ramirez and S. L. Beilock, "Writing about Testing Worries Boosts Exam Performance in the Classroom." *Science* 331, no. 6014 (2011): 211–213.

❖ The journal *Advances in Psychiatric Treatment* presents a detailed review of over eighty studies of the health benefits of expressive writing and a discussion of the possible mechanisms that underlie the observed health benefits. (This review is referred to in chapter 1.) See K. A. Baikie and K. Wilhelm, "Emotional and Physical Health Benefits of Expressive Writing." *Advances in Psychiatric Treatment* 11, no. 5 (2005): 338–346.

❖ Bridget Murray reviews some of the research literature that examines the benefits of writing on the immune system through examining HIV/AIDS patients and patients' responses to the hepatitis B vaccine. See B. Murray, "Writing to Heal." *American Psychological Association* 33, no. 6. (2002): 54.

❖ On each of three consecutive days, 107 asthma and rheumatoid arthritis patients wrote for twenty minutes— seventy-one of them wrote about the most stressful event of their lives and the rest about the emotionally neutral subject of their daily plans. Four months later, seventy patients in the stressful-writing group showed improvement and deteriorated less in objective, clinical evaluations compared with thirty-seven of the control patients. See J. Smyth, A. Stone, A. Hurewitz, and A. Kaell, "Effects of Writing about Stressful Experiences on Symptom Reduction in Patients with Asthma or Rheumatoid Arthritis: A Randomized Trial." *Journal of the American Medical Association* 281, no. 14 (1999): 1304–1309.

❖ A very early study involved forty students at Duke University who were worried about their grades. The intervention group was simply *shown* stories from other students who talked about how it just takes time to adjust to college. The students in this intervention group improved their grade-point averages and were less likely to drop out of school than those in the control group. See T. D. Wilson and P. W. Linville, "Improving the Academic Performance of College Freshmen: Attribution Therapy Revisited." *Journal of Personality and Social Psychology* 42, no. 2 (1982): 367–376.

❖ Dr. James Pennebaker, a psychology professor at the University of Texas, has shown, in study after study, that writing for even fifteen minutes a day about a troubling personal issue or trauma can improve one's overall health. He writes: "People who wrote about their deepest thoughts and feelings surrounding traumatic experiences evidenced heightened immune function compared with those who wrote about superficial topics." Many of Dr. Pennebaker's studies are cited in his book *Opening Up: The Healing Power of Expressing Emotions* (see appendix B).

—ᜑ—

One does not become enlightened by imagining figures of light, but by making the darkness conscious.

—Louise DeSalvo

Appendix B

A Selected Bibliography

There is a crack in everything. That's how the light gets in.
Leonard Cohen

For this bibliography, we have selected books that have been meaningful to us and that we feel would be relevant to you if you are (a) an adult child of an alcoholic and/or an adult child of another manifestation of family dysfunction; (b) interested in exploring and appreciating your past; and (c) interested in writing as a tool for healing and sharing.

There are many, many helpful books, articles, CDs, and organizations that focus on writing, healing, and both specific and general childhood trauma. If you want to explore further, simply use an Internet search tool. You will likely be amazed at the array of helpful resources available.

And if you have favorite resources, we'd love to hear from you so we can expand our list.

Ackerman, Robert J. *Perfect Daughters: Adult Daughters of Alcoholics*. Deerfield Beach, FL: Health Communications, 1989.

This was the first book to examine, exclusively, the effects of an alcoholic parent on daughters. Even though it was first published over twenty-five years ago, the thoughts, ideas, and feelings of the more than 1,200 women surveyed continue to ring true with relevance. The book describes the different impacts of alcoholic mothers versus alcoholic fathers, the common traits of daughters of alcoholics, and how they adapt to and cope with their surroundings, and the author is emphatic that the hundreds of women he interviewed were all survivors, saying, "I am writing about the survival, hope, capabilities, and strengths I have witnessed from adult survivors." Through lists of topics like "lessons learned," snippets of stories, and sage advice, the author conveys both knowledge and compassion.

Adult Children of Alcoholics World Service Organization. *Adult Children of Alcoholic/Dysfunctional Families*. Torrance, CA: Adult Children of Alcoholics World Service Organization, 2006.

A very helpful and detailed book that outlines the history and evolution of the ACA movement and provides useful and provocative material for topic discussions, consideration of the ACA Twelve Steps and Twelve Traditions, as well as stories and reflections about the common traits of adult children of alcoholics, re-parenting, recovery, and how to practice self-love. This book acknowledges that there are many causes of dysfunction in families, not just alcoholism.

Al-Anon Family Groups. *How Al-Anon Works for Families and Friends of Alcoholics*. Virginia Beach, VA: Al-Anon Family Group Headquarters, Inc., 2008.

According to this book's preface, it "invites us in to see how Al-Anon helps families of alcoholics to overcome even the most negative aspects of their lives and, in turn, extend hope and help to others." In addition to reviewing Al-Anon's history and its Twelve Steps, Twelve Traditions, Twelve Concepts of Service, and familiar-sounding slogans, the book is full of personal stories that help the reader "grasp the enormous impact the alcoholism of someone close has had on our physical, emotional, and spiritual well-being."

Beattie, Melody. *The Language of Letting Go: Daily Meditations on Codependency.* Center City, MN: Hazelden, 1990.

This book provides a meditation for every day, each one gently reminding us that the best way to heal and grow is to take responsibility for our own pain and self-care, to let ourselves feel all of our emotions, and to accept our powerlessness.

Brach, Tara. *Radical Acceptance: Embracing Your Life with the Heart of a Buddha.* New York: Bantam Books, 2003.

The author understands that many people have suffered and have adopted habits of crippling self-judgment and a drive to control everything around us. With warmth and clarity, she encourages us to embrace who we are and to fully live in the present. She writes, "When we practice Radical Acceptance, we begin with the fears and wounds of our own life and discover that our heart of compassion widens endlessly . . . As we free ourselves from the suffering of 'something is wrong with me,' we trust and express the fullness of who we are."

Brown, Brené. *The Gifts of Imperfection: Let Go of Who You Think You're Supposed to Be and Embrace Who You Are.* Center City, MN: Hazelden, 2010.

The author encourages everyone to embrace a sense of worthiness, a belief of "I am enough." Looking deeply into the causes of shame and vulnerability, and the dark emotions and experiences that get in the way of leading a fuller life, Brown offers ten guideposts for "Wholehearted Living."

Brown, Brené. *Rising Strong*. New York: Spiegel & Grau, 2015.

The author interviewed a wide range of people who appeared to be successful in their lives and listened to their stories about being brave, falling, and getting back up. The common denominator was that all these people understood the power of emotion and were not afraid to lean into discomfort and learn from it. Building on her previous books, Brown concludes that "rising strong after a fall is how we cultivate wholeheartedness."

Cameron, Julia. *The Artist's Way: A Spiritual Path to Higher Creativity*. New York: Tarcher/Putnam, 1992.

At its core, this book is about a spiritual path, initiated and practiced through creativity. As a key step on the creativity path, Cameron proposes a discipline of "Morning Pages," a practice of writing three pages, longhand, at the beginning of every day—not necessarily about anything in particular. She calls this practice both a brain dump and a doorway to creative recovery.

Cameron, Julia. *The Right to Write: An Invitation and Initiation into the Writing Life*. New York: Tarcher/Putnam, 1998.

The author invites readers to write, explaining "it is human nature to write. Writing claims our world . . . writing brings clarity and passion to the act of living . . . writing is good for the soul." Each of the more than forty chapters includes a specific invitation to write along with a parallel initiation.

DeSalvo, Louise. *Writing as a Way of Healing: How Telling Our Stories Transforms Our Lives*. Boston: Beacon Press, 1999.

Based on twenty years of research about the efficacy of using writing as a restorative tool, the author shows how even famous writers have been transformed by the writing process. The book contains a number of suggestions for writing, along with helpful examples.

Jones, Catherine Ann. *Heal Your Self with Writing*. Studio City, CA: Divine Arts, 2013.

The opening lines of this book are: "Our lives may be determined less by past events than by the way we remember them. If we learn how to reframe the pieces of our past and re-vision our life story so that suffering becomes meaningful, we can radically boost our chances of healing, empowerment, growth, and transformation." Hundreds of compelling exercises will encourage anyone wanting to write.

Klauser, Henriette Anne. *With Pen in Hand: The Healing Power of Writing*. Cambridge, MA: Perseus, 2003.

The author shares stories from people who have used writing to gain perspective about their lives and, for each one, asks the question, "Why write?" The book also outlines various practical writing techniques and encouraging words.

Lesser, Elizabeth. *Broken Open: How Difficult Times Can Help Us Grow*. New York: Villard, 2005.

This book is a combination of stories, humorous insights, and practical suggestions for exploring one's past. The author is the cofounder of the Omega Institute, the world's largest center for spiritual retreat and personal growth, and in that role has met thousands of people who are suffering from one cause or another. She says "the most profound of the tools we have at our disposal is the simple act of telling our stories to other human travellers . . . By sharing our most human traits, we begin to feel less odd, less lonely, and less pessimistic."

Miller, Alice. *The Drama of the Gifted Child: The Search for the True Self*. New York: Basic Books, 2007.

Miller uses the word "gifted" in her title not to refer to smart or talented children but, rather, to refer to anyone who survived an abusive childhood. While she praises such survival, she argues that surviving is not enough and discusses ways to reclaim one's life. "The damage done to us during our childhood cannot be undone," she writes, "since we cannot change anything in our past. We can, however, change ourselves. We can repair ourselves . . . This path is the only route by which we can at last leave behind the cruel, invisible prison of our childhood."

Nepo, Mark. *The Book of Awakening: Having the Life You Want by Being Present to the Life You Have*. San Francisco: Conari Press, 2011.

This book offers a meditation, a reflection, and a question for each day of the year. The collection offers wisdom, clarity, kindness, and enthusiasm for getting the most out of life every day. One can read this book slowly, savoring each day's message, and/or one can use the subject index to go directly to issues and topics of particular interest.

Palmer, Parker J. *A Hidden Wholeness: The Journey Toward an Undivided Life*. San Francisco: Jossey-Bass, 2004.

The author feels that we are living in an era of economic injustice, ecological ruin, and violence in war and that this "blizzard" causes us to feel a sense of fear, frenzy, greed, and indifference to suffering. He offers this book as a way of "tying a rope from the back door out to the barn so that we can find out way home again." The rich text communicates an array of qualities and tools that will reestablish a sense of caring community.

Pennebaker, James W. and John F. Evans. *Expressive Writing: Words That Heal*. Enumclaw, WA: Idyll Arbor, 2014.

This book is an excellent general reference on expressive writing, outlining its various beneficial biological, psychological, and behavioral effects based on over three hundred studies, as well as various approaches to techniques for how to do it.

Pennebaker, James W. *Opening Up: The Healing Power of Expressing Emotions*. New York: The Guilford Press, 1997.

This book summarizes ten years of research on the positive connection of writing about deeply troubling and emotionally difficult events and positive changes in both brain and immune functions.

Remen, Rachel Naomi. *Kitchen Table Wisdom: Stories That Heal*. New York: Riverhead Books, 1996, 2006.

The author is a physician, professor of medicine, therapist, and long-term survivor of chronic illness and, in this book, shares a collection of true stories—what she calls "kitchen table wisdom"—based on the human tradition of shared experience. She says, "Facts bring us to knowledge; stories bring us to wisdom."

*You're braver than you believe, stronger than
you seem, and smarter than you think.*

—Christopher Robin (A. A. Milne)

About the Authors

Liz Crocker

Liz Crocker's career has included teaching, broadcasting, writing, and running several businesses. She currently owns Canada's oldest children's bookstore, which she cofounded in 1978, and holds leadership positions with a number of health care and cultural organizations. Liz is the author of two children's books and hundreds of chapters and articles in books, magazines, and newspapers. With Bev Johnson, Liz coauthored *Privileged Presence: Personal Stories of Connections in Health Care*, published in 2006 with a second edition in 2014. She also edited *The Healing Circle: Integrating Science, Wisdom, and Compassion in Reclaiming Wholeness on the Cancer Journey*, published in 2010.

Polly Bennell

Polly Bennell has worked in publishing, advertising, and education; has been an independent filmmaker; practiced psychotherapy; and taught writing and film at the university level. She currently maintains a life-coaching practice for writers, among others, and also practices writing herself.

Holly Book

Holly Book's path has taken her on an amazing journey of motherhood, owning businesses, and being the editor of a children's magazine. Holly eventually attended seminary and became a hospice chaplain. For the last ten years, she and her husband have been ministering to the homeless and those struggling with addiction on the streets of Atlanta.

A Special Note

We would love to hear from you if you give writing a try. We were able to support each other as we travelled some of these bumpy roads and we'd love to support you, too, and celebrate whatever discoveries you experience.

You can write us c/o Bull Publishing, P.O. Box 1377
Boulder, Colorado, 80306 USA Or send us
an email at lizcrocker@eastlink.ca

Index